# Mammoth
# Math
# Workbook

# Mammoth Math Workbook

(with a little help from some elephant shrews)

## David Macaulay

**DK**

**Produced for DK by**
**Just Content Limited**
10A Little Square, Braintree, Essex, CM7 1UT

**Editorial Partner** Just Content Limited
**Design Partner** emc design ltd.
**Consultant** Branka Surla

**DK London**
**Senior Editor** Michelle Crane
**Senior US Editor** Kayla Dugger
**Executive US Editor** Lori Cates Hand
**Project Art Editor** Kit Lane
**Senior Jacket Designer** Suhita Dharamjit
**DTP Designer** Rakesh Kumar
**Senior Jackets Coordinator** Priyanka Sharma Saddi
**Jackets Design Development Manager** Sophia MTT
**Production Editor** Gillian Reid
**Production Controller** Jack Matts
**Managing Editor** Francesca Baines
**Managing Art Editor** Philip Letsu
**Publisher** Andrew Macintyre
**Art Director** Karen Self
**Associate Publishing Director** Liz Wheeler
**Publishing Director** Jonathan Metcalf

First American Edition, 2024
Published in the United States by DK Publishing,
a division of Penguin Random House LLC
1745 Broadway, 20th Floor, New York, NY 10019

A catalog record for this book
is available from the Library of Congress.
ISBN 978-0-5938-4273-7

Printed and bound in China

**www.dk.com**

MIX
Paper | Supporting
responsible forestry
FSC™ C018179

This book was made with Forest
Stewardship Council™ certified
paper—one small step in DK's
commitment to a sustainable future.
Learn more at **www.dk.com/uk/
information/sustainability**

# Contents

# Counting and number symbols

Before writing or number systems existed, people used methods like counting on fingers or toes. Being able to count is important in everyday life.

The elephant shrews have discovered that the ancient Romans used the letters I, V, X, L, C, D, and M in their number system. Can you help the shrews work out what letters were used for numbers 1 to 10?

| | | | | | | | | | |
|---|---|---|---|---|---|---|---|---|---|
| Ones | I 1 | II 2 | III 3 | IV 4 | V 5 | VI 6 | VII 7 | VIII 8 | IX 9 |
| Tens | X 10 | XX 20 | XXX 30 | XL 40 | L 50 | LX 60 | LXX 70 | LXXX 80 | XC 90 |
| Hundreds | C 100 | CC 200 | CCC 300 | CD 400 | D 500 | DC 600 | DCC 700 | DCCC 800 | CM 900 |
| Thousands | M 1,000 | MM 2,000 | MMM 3,000 | I̅V̅ 4,000 | V̅ 5,000 | V̅I̅ 6,000 | V̅I̅I̅ 7,000 | V̅I̅I̅I̅ 8,000 | I̅X̅ 9,000 |

Draw lines to match the Roman numerals with the numbers they represent.

| V | III | VII | I | X | II | VIII | IV | IX | VI |
|---|---|---|---|---|---|---|---|---|---|

| 1 | 2 | 3 | 4 | 5 | 6 | 7 | 8 | 9 | 10 |
|---|---|---|---|---|---|---|---|---|---|

(1) Write the number of elephant shrews as a number and as a Roman numeral.

a)   Number ☐

Roman numeral ☐

b)   Number ☐

Roman numeral ☐

6

# Number systems

Many number systems have been invented throughout history, each with their own set of rules. The number system we use today was invented in India more than 1,000 years ago.

**Ancient Greek**
The letters of the alphabet used to stand for numbers, too.

**Ancient Roman**
Letters were also used to make numbers.

**Ancient Chinese**
Each number from 1 to 10 had its own symbol, and there were different symbols for multiples of 10.

**Hindu–Arabic**
This is the world's most common system. It is different from those that came before it because it has the symbol zero (0).

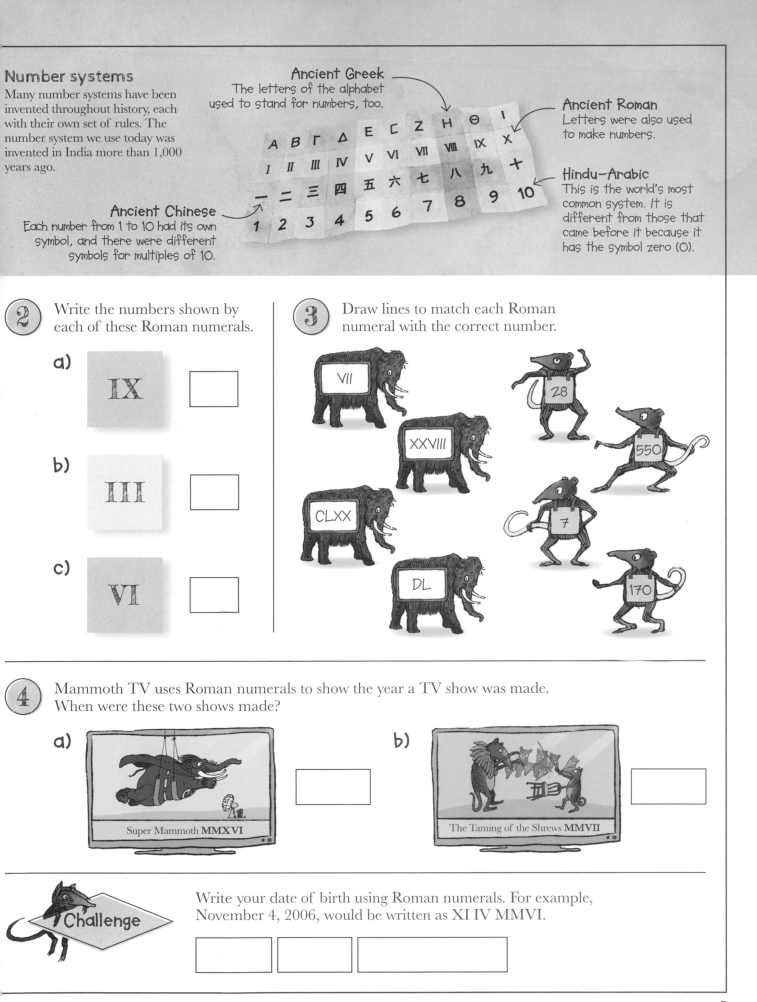

2) Write the numbers shown by each of these Roman numerals.

a) IX □

b) III □

c) VI □

3) Draw lines to match each Roman numeral with the correct number.

VII

XXVIII

CLXX

DL

28

550

7

170

4) Mammoth TV uses Roman numerals to show the year a TV show was made. When were these two shows made?

a) Super Mammoth **MMXVI** □

b) The Taming of the Shrews **MMVII** □

**Challenge**

Write your date of birth using Roman numerals. For example, November 4, 2006, would be written as XI IV MMVI.

□ □ □

# Zero

Although zero means "nothing," it plays an important role in math. It is essential to our number system, and we use it in everyday life—to keep score in a sports contest, to take a temperature, and when we tell the time.

A temperature of 0° on the thermometer describes a value on the scale. It doesn't mean there is no temperature!

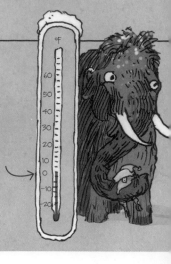

Warm-up Can you help the mammoths show the elephant shrews why zero is different from other numbers by drawing the number of mammoths left after these calculations?

Zero mammoths here!

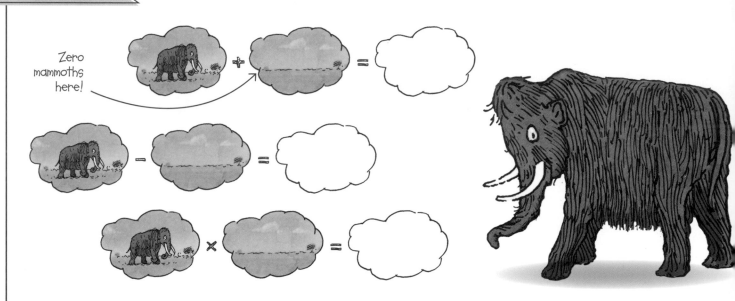

## Practice

① For each of the number sentences below involving zero, work out the answer.

a)  3 + 0 = ☐        c)  50 + 0 = ☐        e)  5 - 0 = ☐        g)  58 - 0 = ☐

b)  7 + 0 = ☐        d)  550 + 0 = ☐       f)  17 - 0 = ☐        h)  475 - 0 = ☐

② Work out the answers to these number sentences.

a)  33 - 33 = ☐                    c)  283 - 283 = ☐

b)  142 - 142 = ☐                  d)  567 - 567 = ☐

## Taking measurements

Zero is a set amount that has its own value when we measure things like temperature.

## Zero on a number line

On the number line, zero has its own place. It is the dividing point between positive and negative numbers.

## Calculating with zero

Zero is different from other numbers in calculations. You can add, subtract, and multiply with zero, but you can't divide by it.

$$8 + 0 = 8$$
$$8 - 0 = 8$$
$$8 \times 0 = 0$$
$$8 \div 0 = ????$$

There is no answer that would make sense here.

$$-4 \quad -3 \quad -2 \quad -1 \quad 0 \quad 1 \quad 2 \quad 3 \quad 4$$

 **3** Fill in the missing numbers in these calculations.

Think about what you need to take away from something to leave nothing at the end.

a) $132 - \boxed{\phantom{00}} = 0$

b) $482 - \boxed{\phantom{00}} = 0$

c) $1,065 - \boxed{\phantom{00}} = 0$

d) $\boxed{\phantom{00}} - 265 = 0$

e) $\boxed{\phantom{00}} - 356 = 0$

f) $\boxed{\phantom{00}} - 672 = 0$

 **4** Look at these number sentences and see if you can work out the answers. The first one has been done for you.

a) $233 + 50 - 50 = \boxed{233}$

b) $435 + 68 - 68 = \boxed{\phantom{00}}$

c) $597 + 76 - 76 = \boxed{\phantom{00}}$

d) $832 + 98 - 98 = \boxed{\phantom{00}}$

**5** Look at these number sentences and see if you can work out the answers. The first one has been done for you.

a) $3 \times 0 = \boxed{0}$

b) $7 \times 0 = \boxed{\phantom{00}}$

c) $52 \times 0 = \boxed{\phantom{00}}$

d) $650 \times 0 = \boxed{\phantom{00}}$

 Challenge

The temperature on this thermometer is 0°. What will the temperature be if it:

a) increases by 10°? $\boxed{\phantom{00}}$

b) decreases by 5°? $\boxed{\phantom{00}}$

9

# Place value

Numbers are made up of symbols called digits. We use the digits 0–9 in our number system, but the value of these digits can change. The value of a digit depends on its position in the number. This is called place value.

Warm-up

Mammoths and elephant shrews are sorting the apples into sets of 10 in the apple packing plant, but they aren't sure how many they have packed so far. Help them by filling in the number of pallets, trays, tubes, and single apples on the boards to give the total. The first one has been done for you.

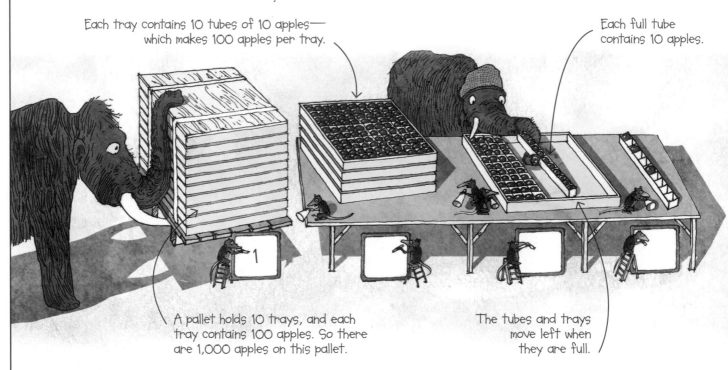

Each tray contains 10 tubes of 10 apples—which makes 100 apples per tray.

Each full tube contains 10 apples.

A pallet holds 10 trays, and each tray contains 100 apples. So there are 1,000 apples on this pallet.

The tubes and trays move left when they are full.

Practice

1 How many apples can you count?

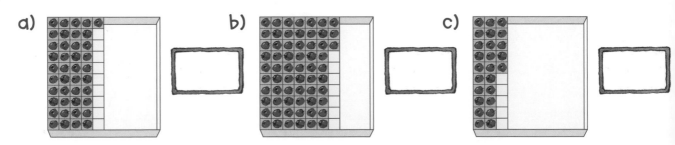

a)

b)

c)

10

# Position matters
The value of the digits in these numbers changes according to their position.

In the number 23, the "2" digit is worth 2 lots of 10.

**23**

The "3" digit is worth 3 ones.

In the number 234, the "2" digit is worth 2 lots of 100.

**234**

The "3" digit is worth 3 lots of 10.

# The special role of zero
Zero has a special job in the place value system. It shows when a place is empty. In the number 2,034, there are no hundreds. Zero is holding the place to make sure all the other numbers have their correct values.

Thousands  Hundreds  Tens  Ones

**2 0 3 4**

Without the zero, this would become 234—a very different number!

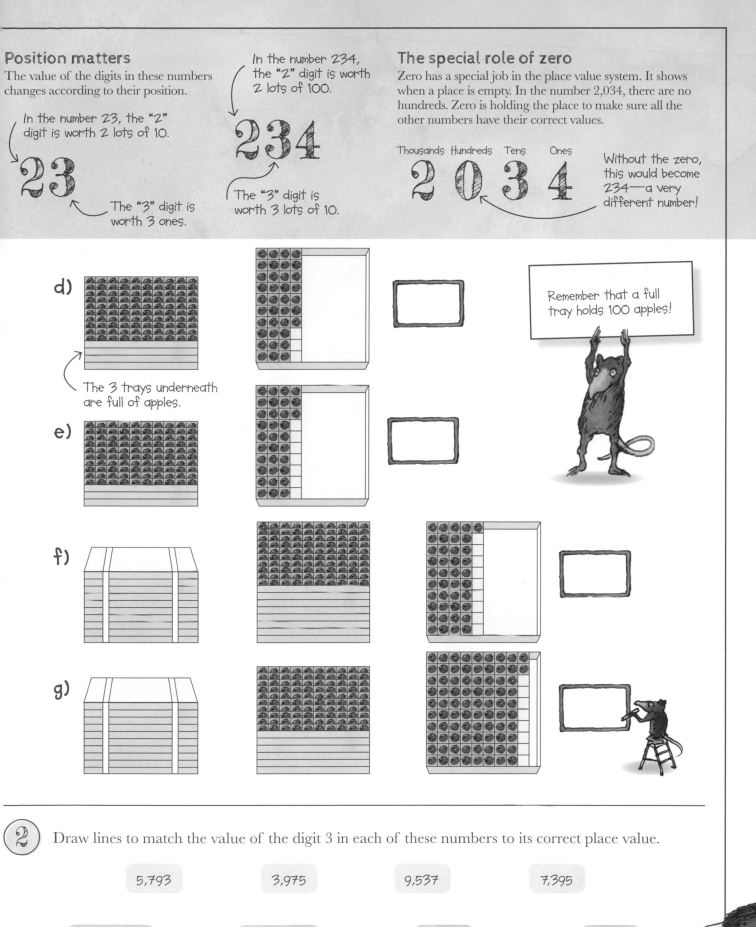

d)

Remember that a full tray holds 100 apples!

The 3 trays underneath are full of apples.

e)

f)

g)

---

② Draw lines to match the value of the digit 3 in each of these numbers to its correct place value.

5,793          3,975          9,537          7,395

3 thousands          3 hundreds          3 ones          3 tens

**3** Help the elephant shrews by writing in the correct numbers on their boards.

Remember that zero shows when a place is empty.

**4** Circle the digit that shows the tens in each number. The first one has been done for you.

a) 7①2

b) 9 5

c) 8 0 4

d) 2,0 7 3

**5** These numbers all contain the digit 4, but it has a different value in each one. Draw lines to match each digit 4 with its correct place value. The first one has been done for you.

a) 4,0 8 2

b) 5,9 0 4

c) 7,0 4 7

d) 3,4 5 0

40

4,000

400

4

**6** Write down the number of apples being described in each of these sentences. The first one has been done for you.

a) 2 hundreds, 0 ones, 3 tens, and 2 thousands.

2,230

b) 0 tens, 6 thousands, 5 hundreds, and 9 ones.

c) 0 ones, 2 thousands, 8 tens, and 1 hundred.

d) 3 thousands, 4 ones, 0 hundreds, and 7 tens.

e) 9 ones, 0 thousands, 6 tens, and 2 hundreds.

f) 4 hundreds, 0 ones, 8 thousands, and 0 tens.

g) 5 ones, 0 thousands, 7 hundreds, and 1 ten.

**7** Circle the elephant shrews holding up the number of apples that have the digit 3 in the hundreds column.

390    4,503    483    538    8,302    2,360

**Challenge**

What is the value of the digit 8 in each of these numbers?

a) 180 [ ]    b) 8,907 [ ]    c) 28 [ ]

# Ordering and comparing numbers

To put numbers in order, we compare their most significant digit—the one with the highest place value. If these are the same, we carry on comparing digits from left to right.

Most significant digit

27,002

Second most significant digit

Warm-up

To crown the winner of this hotly contested talent show, the judges must carefully compare the scores. Put the scores onto the scoreboard in the correct order. Take care— you don't want to declare the wrong contestant the winner!

Highest score

Lowest score

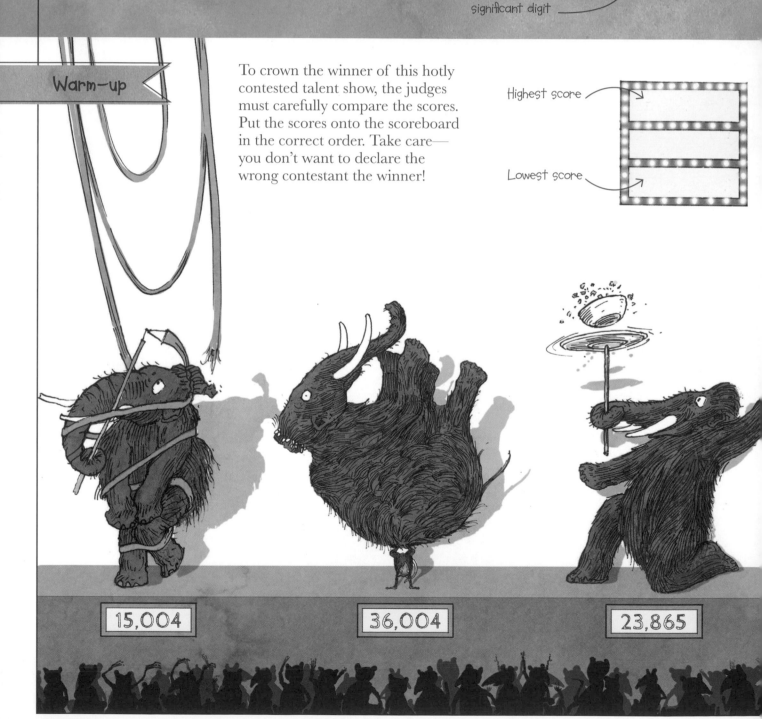

15,004

36,004

23,865

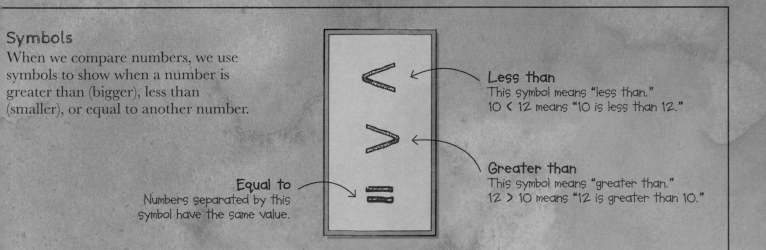

## Symbols

When we compare numbers, we use symbols to show when a number is greater than (bigger), less than (smaller), or equal to another number.

**Less than**
This symbol means "less than."
10 < 12 means "10 is less than 12."

**Greater than**
This symbol means "greater than."
12 > 10 means "12 is greater than 10."

**Equal to**
Numbers separated by this symbol have the same value.

## Practice

1 Use the correct symbol to compare these pairs of numbers. The first one has been done for you.

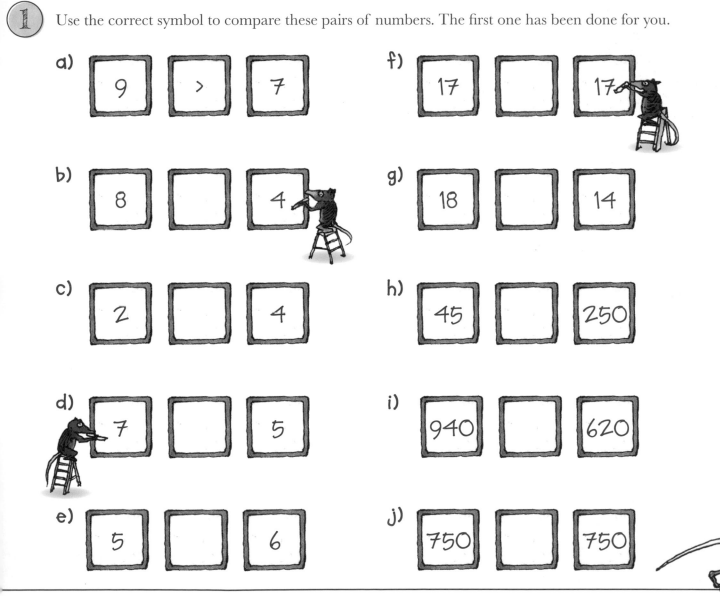

a) 9 > 7

b) 8 ☐ 4

c) 2 ☐ 4

d) 7 ☐ 5

e) 5 ☐ 6

f) 17 ☐ 17

g) 18 ☐ 14

h) 45 ☐ 250

i) 940 ☐ 620

j) 750 ☐ 750

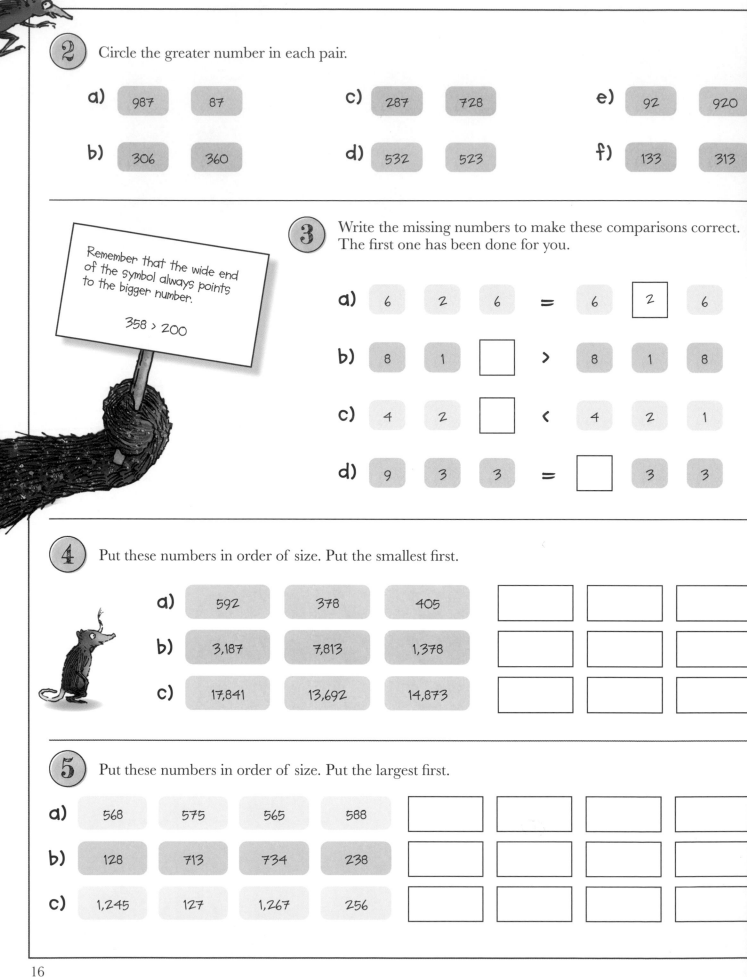

**2** Circle the greater number in each pair.

a) 987    87

b) 306    360

c) 287    728

d) 532    523

e) 92    920

f) 133    313

Remember that the wide end of the symbol always points to the bigger number.

358 > 200

**3** Write the missing numbers to make these comparisons correct. The first one has been done for you.

a)  6    2    6    =    6    [2]    6

b)  8    1    [ ]    >    8    1    8

c)  4    2    [ ]    <    4    2    1

d)  9    3    3    =    [ ]    3    3

**4** Put these numbers in order of size. Put the smallest first.

a)  592    378    405    [ ]  [ ]  [ ]

b)  3,187    7,813    1,378    [ ]  [ ]  [ ]

c)  17,841    13,692    14,873    [ ]  [ ]  [ ]

**5** Put these numbers in order of size. Put the largest first.

a)  568    575    565    588    [ ]  [ ]  [ ]  [ ]

b)  128    713    734    238    [ ]  [ ]  [ ]  [ ]

c)  1,245    127    1,267    256    [ ]  [ ]  [ ]  [ ]

**6** The elephant shrews split into teams to play a game. They are now comparing their scores to work out which team has won. Order the teams by their scores. Start with the highest.

| | |
|---|---|
| Blue team | 6,957 |
| Red team | 6,839 |
| Purple team | 6,965 |
| Green team | 6,841 |
| Yellow team | 6,941 |
| Orange team | 5,742 |

| | | | | | |
|---|---|---|---|---|---|

**7** The elephant shrew has friends that live in different parts of the country. Order the friends by their distance from the shrew, starting with the nearest. The first one has been done for you.

200 km   5 km   1,040 km   14 km   102 km

| 5 km | | | | |
|---|---|---|---|---|

**Challenge** Choose numbers from the boxes to fit the blanks to make these comparisons true.

12,001   10,902   14,820   10,999

a) 11,003 > [ ] > 10,987

b) 10,845 < [ ] < 10,950

c) 12,021 > [ ] > 11,987

d) 15,752 > [ ] > 14,566

17

# Rounding

Rounding a number by changing it to another one that is close in value but easier to work with helps you add, subtract, or multiply numbers in your head. To round to the nearest 10, look at the ones digit. To round to the nearest 100, look at the tens digit.

When a digit is less than 5, we round down. When it's 5 or more, we round up.

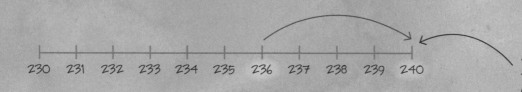

236 rounded to the nearest ten is 240, because 236 is closer to 240 than 230.

Warm-up

The elephant shrews are using the roller coaster to help the mammoths remember the rounding rule. Can you answer the questions to help them?

These numbers all roll forward to the ten ahead.

These numbers don't quite make it past the peak. They slide backward to the ten before.

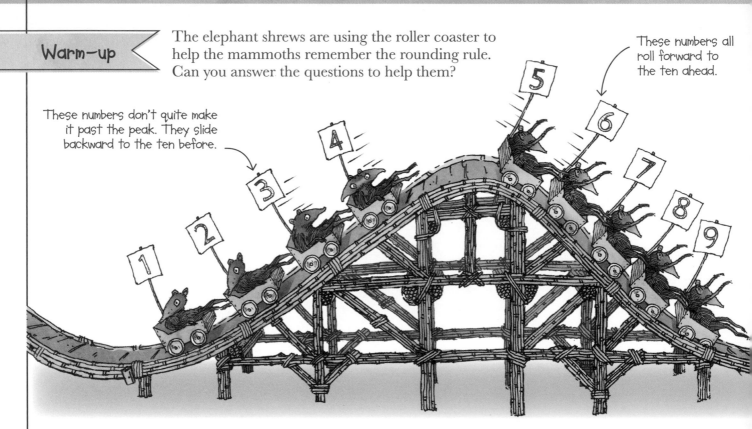

## Rounding down

a) What digits round down?

b) What does 82 round down to?

c) What does 162 round down to?

## Rounding up

d) What digits round up?

e) What does 26 round up to?

f) What does 349 round up to?

18

**1** This muddled mammoth wants to round 65 to the nearest 10. What is the correct rounded number? ☐

**2** What are the following numbers rounded to the nearest 10?

**a)** 58 ☐  **b)** 43 ☐  **c)** 27 ☐  **d)** 79 ☐

**3** Follow the instructions below when rounding to the nearest 10.

**a)** Circle the five numbers below that round to 240 when rounded to the nearest 10.

235    238    242    233    244    239    246

**b)** Circle the four numbers below that round to 2,000 when rounded to the nearest 10.

1,998    2,011    2,002    1,996    1,992    2,007    2,003

**4** Round these numbers to the nearest 100.

**a)** 132 ☐       **c)** 245 ☐

**b)** 276 ☐       **d)** 145 ☐

When rounding to the nearest hundred, look at the tens digit instead.

The tens digit is 3, so we round down.

The tens digit is 6, so we round up.

**5** Circle the numbers that round to 8,000 when rounded to the nearest 100.

8,121        8,023        7,552

7,972        7,098        8,952

**Challenge**

Round these numbers to the nearest 1,000.

**a)** 4,823 ☐       **b)** 5,378 ☐       **c)** 6,247 ☐

# Estimating

Sometimes it can be useful to make an estimate, or sensible guess, for a number, especially when very big numbers are involved or you have lots of objects that would take too long to count. Estimates can also help when checking calculations to make sure the answer you get is similar to your rough guess.

Warm-up

The mammoths are struggling to count this group of elephant shrews, who are jumping around. Can you fill in the blanks below to help them make a sensible guess?

There are _____ shrews in the front row and 5 uneven rows. The number of shrews is _____ × 5 = _____.

You can count the number of shrews in one row, then multiply by the number of rows.

Practice

**1** Estimate how many elephant shrews there are in the crowd. Each square contains 10 shrews.

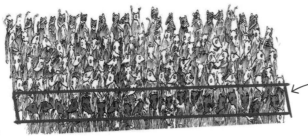

a) [   ]    b) [   ]    c) [   ]

**2** Estimate the value that the arrow points to on these number lines.

a) 
```
0                              1,000
```
[   ]

b)
```
0  100 200 300 400 500 600 700 800 900 1,000
```
[   ]

**3** Draw four arrows to show the position of these numbers on the number line.

```
0                                    10,000
```

a) 2,500    b) 4,500    c) 7,500    d) 9,500

## Using a grid

You can use a grid to estimate the total number of a large group. Divide the group into equal imaginary squares, count the total in one square, and then multiply by the total number of squares.

There are 8 shrews in the highlighted square.

Multiply 8 by 15 (the number of squares) and you get an estimate of 120 shrews.

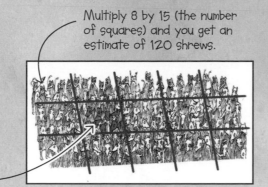

## Using a number line

You can use a number line to make estimates. The arrow is about halfway on the line. Half of 100 is 50, so an estimate for the value shown is 50.

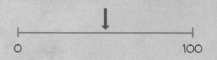

0                                    100

---

**4** The elephant shrews want to see if they can afford some snacks. Round the prices up or down to the nearest 50¢ to give an estimate of the rough cost.

**a)** The popcorn costs about $ ☐

**b)** The drink is about $ ☐

**c)** The ice cream is about $ ☐

**d)** The estimate of the total cost is $ ☐ + $ ☐ + $ ☐ = $ ☐

---

**5** Estimate to the nearest 50¢ how much it would cost to buy each of these combinations.

**a)**
$2.30   $1.90

☐

**b)**
$2.75   $1.45

☐

**c)**
$2.10   $1.75   $2.10

☐

---

 **Challenge**

Estimate to the nearest 50¢ how much it would cost to buy these snacks.

$2.10   $2.10   $1.75   $1.75   $2.10   $2.10

☐

# Addition

Putting two or more quantities together to make a bigger quantity is called addition. There are different ways to do addition: counting all and counting on.

## Counting all

In counting all, you put all the amounts to be added into one group and count them all.

There are 2 purple balloons in one group.

There is 1 yellow balloon in the other group.

Putting them all together makes one group to count. There are 3 balloons in total.

Warm-up

The mammoths are trying to explain how to write an addition sentence to the elephant shrews. Help them by filling in the missing symbols.

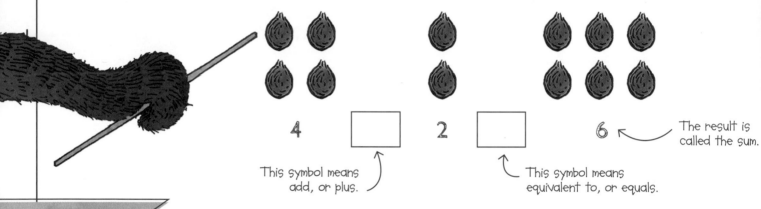

4 [ ]  2 [ ]  6 ← The result is called the sum.

This symbol means add, or plus.

This symbol means equivalent to, or equals.

## Practice

1  How many balloons is each elephant shrew or mammoth holding? Count them all to find out.

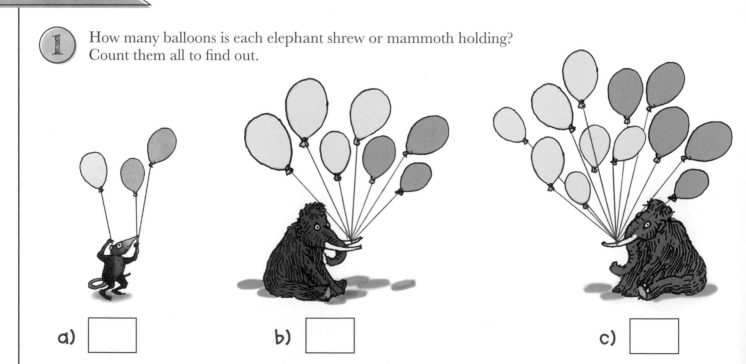

a) [ ]

b) [ ]

c) [ ]

## Counting on

In counting on, you start with one number and count forward the number of places you need to add. The number line below shows that starting from 6 and adding 3 more will make 9.

## Writing down addition

We write addition sentences using the "+" or "add" symbol to show when numbers are being added together. The "=" or "equals" symbol means equivalent to.

Start counting from the largest number.

A number line can help count on.

6 + 3 = 9 coconuts

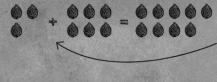

We can add numbers in any order.

Swapping the order the numbers are added in gives the same total.

**2** How many coconuts? Count on to find out.

a)

15 + 2 = ☐

b)

103 + 4 = ☐

We use the counting on method with number lines.

**3** Use this number line to add these numbers together.

1  2  3  4  5  6  7  8  9  10  11  12  13  14  15  16  17  18  19  20

a) 4 + 9 = ☐   b) 5 + 11 = ☐   c) 9 + 9 = ☐

**4** Use this number line to add these numbers together.

150  151  152  153  154  155  156  157  158  159  160  161  162  163  164  165  166  167  168  169  170

a) 152 + 5 = ☐   b) 154 + 8 = ☐   c) 157 + 11 = ☐

23

**5** The mammoths have started running a bus route to take the elephant shrews from their burrows to their feeding ground. They use this number line to help them work out how many shrews they have on each bus.

**a)** There are 6 shrews on the yellow bus.
3 more get on. How many are on the bus now? ☐

**b)** There are 13 shrews on the red bus.
6 more get on. How many are on the bus now? ☐

**c)** There are 4 shrews on the green bus.
9 more get on. How many are on the bus now? ☐

**6** Draw lines to match each addition question with the correct answer.
Use the number line to help you.

| 11 + 5 | 12 + 2 | 16 + 8 | 13 + 13 | 17 + 5 | 18 + 7 | 22 + 5 |

| 22 | 24 | 25 | 14 | 16 | 26 | 27 |

**7** Use this number line to add these numbers together.

**a)** 1,212 + 4 = ☐

**b)** 1,202 + 6 = ☐

**c)** 1,207 + 7 = ☐

**d)** 1,204 + 5 = ☐

**e)** 1,202 + 4 = ☐

**f)** 1,209 + 6 = ☐

**g)** 1,210 + 7 = ☐

**h)** 1,214 + 5 = ☐

Number lines can help you with addition sentences even for large numbers.

**8** You can use number lines to add larger numbers. Use this number line to add these numbers together by making jumps of 10.

| | | | | | | | | | | | | | | | | | | | | |
|0|10|20|30|40|50|60|70|80|90|100|110|120|130|140|150|160|170|180|190|200|

a) 20 + 10 = ☐

b) 30 + 30 = ☐

c) 110 + 50 = ☐

d) 140 + 60 = ☐

**9** Use this number grid to help you answer these addition questions.

For larger numbers, we can use a number grid to help us with addition. We can count on from one number to find the answer.

a) 34 + 22 = ☐

b) 21 + 25 = ☐

c) 63 + 15 = ☐

d) 89 + 11 = ☐

e) 8 + 67 = ☐

f) 49 + 39 = ☐

| 1 | 2 | 3 | 4 | 5 | 6 | 7 | 8 | 9 | 10 |
|---|---|---|---|---|---|---|---|---|---|
| 11 | 12 | 13 | 14 | 15 | 16 | 17 | 18 | 19 | 20 |
| 21 | 22 | 23 | 24 | 25 | 26 | 27 | 28 | 29 | 30 |
| 31 | 32 | 33 | 34 | 35 | 36 | 37 | 38 | 39 | 40 |
| 41 | 42 | 43 | 44 | 45 | 46 | 47 | 48 | 49 | 50 |
| 51 | 52 | 53 | 54 | 55 | 56 | 57 | 58 | 59 | 60 |
| 61 | 62 | 63 | 64 | 65 | 66 | 67 | 68 | 69 | 70 |
| 71 | 72 | 73 | 74 | 75 | 76 | 77 | 78 | 79 | 80 |
| 81 | 82 | 83 | 84 | 85 | 86 | 87 | 88 | 89 | 90 |
| 91 | 92 | 93 | 94 | 95 | 96 | 97 | 98 | 99 | 100 |

Challenge

The mammoths are competing to knock down coconuts. The first mammoth knocks down 12 coconuts, the second mammoth knocks down 5 coconuts, the third mammoth knocks down 8 coconuts, and the fourth mammoth knocks down 3 coconuts. How many coconuts do they knock down in total?

☐ + ☐ + ☐ + ☐ = ☐

# Subtraction

Subtraction is the inverse of addition. It is where we take away one number from another to find out what's left. You can think about subtraction as counting back or as finding the difference between two numbers.

## Counting back

In counting back, you start with one number and count back the number of places you need to subtract. The number line below shows that starting from 6 and taking away 2 will leave 4

To subtract 2 from 6, count back 2 from right to left.

-2

---

**Warm-up**

The mammoth is trying their luck at knocking down coconuts but isn't sure if there are enough rocks left to knock down the remaining coconuts. Help the mammoth work out how many rocks and coconuts are left.

The mammoth started with a full box of 9 rocks.

**a)** How many rocks has the mammoth thrown?

**b)** What is the difference between the number of rocks the mammoth had to start with and the number that have been thrown?

☐ − ☐ = ☐

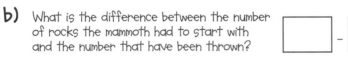

There were 6 coconuts to start with.

**c)** How many coconuts has the mammoth knocked off?

**d)** What is the difference between the number of coconuts to start with and the number that have been knocked off?

☐ − ☐ = ☐

## Finding the difference

The shrews started with 5 cotton candy sticks but have eaten 2. There are 3 left, so the difference between 5 and 2 is 3.

5 − 2 = 3

## Writing down subtraction

Unlike addition, in subtraction number sentences, you can't switch the order of the numbers you are subtracting without getting a different result: 9 − 2 is not the same as 2 − 9.

9        −     2     =        7

Subtraction number sentences use the "−" or "subtract" symbol to show when one number is being taken away from another.

## Practice

**1** Count back along the coconut pedestals to work out these subtractions.

a) 6 − 3 = ☐

b) 6 − 5 = ☐

c) 6 − 2 = ☐

d) 6 − 1 = ☐

**2** Use the balloons to help you answer these subtraction calculations.

a) 9 − 4 = ☐    c) 9 − 5 = ☐    e) 9 − 1 = ☐

b) 9 − 6 = ☐    d) 9 − 2 = ☐    f) 9 − 3 = ☐

**3** Use this number line to help you answer these subtraction calculations.

1    2    3    4    5    6    7    8    9    10

a) 10 − 3 = ☐        c) 10 − 7 = ☐        e) 10 − 6 = ☐

b) 10 − 1 = ☐        d) 10 − 9 = ☐        f) 10 − 5 = ☐

**4** Use this number line to answer these subtraction calculations.

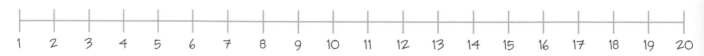

1  2  3  4  5  6  7  8  9  10  11  12  13  14  15  16  17  18  19  20

**a)** 20 – 3 = ☐

**b)** 20 – 7 = ☐

**c)** 20 – 9 = ☐

**d)** 20 – 5 = ☐

**e)** 15 – 5 = ☐

**f)** 18 – 6 = ☐

---

**5** Use this number line to answer these subtraction calculations.

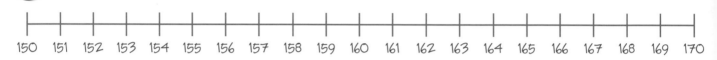

150  151  152  153  154  155  156  157  158  159  160  161  162  163  164  165  166  167  168  169  170

**a)** 170 – 8 = ☐

**b)** 160 – 3 = ☐

**c)** 164 – 2 = ☐

**d)** 154 – 4 = ☐

**e)** 167 – 3 = ☐

**f)** 162 – 12 = ☐

---

**6** Use this number line to answer these subtraction calculations.

1,200  1,201  1,202  1,203  1,204  1,205  1,206  1,207  1,208  1,209  1,210  1,211  1,212  1,213  1,214  1,215  1,216  1,217  1,218  1,219  1,220

**a)** 1,220 – 4 = ☐

**b)** 1,218 – 10 = ☐

**c)** 1,217 – 3 = ☐

**d)** 1,210 – 5 = ☐

**e)** 1,213 – 9 = ☐

**f)** 1,220 – 7 = ☐

**g)** 1,208 – 5 = ☐

**h)** 1,220 – 14 = ☐

**i)** 1,218 – 13 = ☐

**j)** 1,219 – 13 = ☐

**k)** 1,217 – 15 = ☐

**l)** 1,220 – 19 = ☐

**m)** 1,220 – 17 = ☐

**n)** 1,218 – 14 = ☐

**7** Use the number grid to help you answer these subtraction calculations.

| 1 | 2 | 3 | 4 | 5 | 6 | 7 | 8 | 9 | 10 |
|---|---|---|---|---|---|---|---|---|---|
| 11 | 12 | 13 | 14 | 15 | 16 | 17 | 18 | 19 | 20 |
| 21 | 22 | 23 | 24 | 25 | 26 | 27 | 28 | 29 | 30 |
| 31 | 32 | 33 | 34 | 35 | 36 | 37 | 38 | 39 | 40 |
| 41 | 42 | 43 | 44 | 45 | 46 | 47 | 48 | 49 | 50 |
| 51 | 52 | 53 | 54 | 55 | 56 | 57 | 58 | 59 | 60 |
| 61 | 62 | 63 | 64 | 65 | 66 | 67 | 68 | 69 | 70 |
| 71 | 72 | 73 | 74 | 75 | 76 | 77 | 78 | 79 | 80 |
| 81 | 82 | 83 | 84 | 85 | 86 | 87 | 88 | 89 | 90 |
| 91 | 92 | 93 | 94 | 95 | 96 | 97 | 98 | 99 | 100 |

To help us subtract larger numbers, we can use a number grid. We can count back from one number to find the answer.

**a)** 87 − 29 = ☐

**b)** 63 − 37 = ☐

**c)** 24 − 11 = ☐

**d)** 54 − 18 = ☐

**e)** 67 − 12 = ☐   **h)** 87 − 78 = ☐

**f)** 56 − 43 = ☐   **i)** 65 − 34 = ☐

**g)** 76 − 14 = ☐   **j)** 36 − 21 = ☐

---

**8** 100 elephant shrews went to a party. Some went home early.
How many were left if …

**a)** 40 went home early? ☐

**b)** 20 went home early? ☐

**c)** 10 went home early? ☐

**d)** 50 went home early? ☐

---

Challenge

Can you help the elephant shrews find the missing numbers in these number sentences?

**a)** 92 − 1☐ = 79   **d)** 84 − ☐3 = 51

**b)** 48 − 22 = ☐6   **e)** 57 − 18 = ☐9

**c)** ☐4 − 16 = 48   **f)** 7☐ − 42 = 33

# Number bonds

Number bonds are pairs of numbers that can be added together to make another number. Knowing the number bonds to 10 is especially useful and can help with addition and subtraction. You can also add zeros to find the number bonds to multiples of 10 or 100.

Warm-up

The elephant shrews are floating in the swimming pool. They want to rearrange themselves into two equal groups to explain how number bonds work to their mammoth friends. Draw around the shrews to make two groups and then fill in the gaps.

There are two equal groups of _____ shrews. There are _____ shrews in total.

A number sentence to show this number bond is 5 + _____ = _____

Practice

**1** Which number bonds to 10 are shown here?

a)

☐ + ☐ = 10

b)

☐ + ☐ = 10

**2** Which number bonds to 20 are shown here?

a)

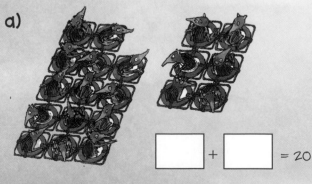

☐ + ☐ = 20

b)

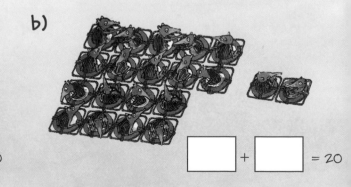

☐ + ☐ = 20

# Number bonds to 10

The number bonds to 10 are the pairs of numbers that can be added together to equal 10. These are $10 + 0, 9 + 1, 8 + 2, 7 + 3, 6 + 4$, and $5 + 5$.

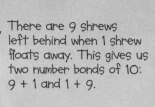
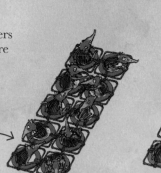

Ten shrews float together in one group. $10 + 0$ is a number bond of 10, and so is $0 + 10$.

There are 9 shrews left behind when 1 shrew floats away. This gives us two number bonds of 10: $9 + 1$ and $1 + 9$.

**3** Complete these number sentences for number bonds to 10.

a) $2 + \boxed{\phantom{0}} = 10$    c) $4 + \boxed{\phantom{0}} = 10$    e) $10 - \boxed{\phantom{0}} = 1$

b) $6 + \boxed{\phantom{0}} = 10$    d) $8 + \boxed{\phantom{0}} = 10$    f) $10 - \boxed{\phantom{0}} = 7$

You can use number bonds for subtraction as well as addition. For example, knowing that 6 and 4 are an addition pair means you also know that $10 - 6 = 4$ and that $10 - 4 = 6$.

**4** Complete these number sentences for number bonds to 20.

a) $13 + \boxed{\phantom{0}} = 20$    c) $12 + \boxed{\phantom{0}} = 20$    e) $20 - \boxed{\phantom{0}} = 5$

b) $17 + \boxed{\phantom{0}} = 20$    d) $2 + \boxed{\phantom{0}} = 20$    f) $20 - \boxed{\phantom{0}} = 16$

**5** Complete these number sentences for number bonds to 100.

a) $90 + \boxed{\phantom{0}} = 100$    c) $20 + \boxed{\phantom{0}} = 100$    e) $100 - \boxed{\phantom{0}} = 70$

b) $50 + \boxed{\phantom{0}} = 100$    d) $60 + \boxed{\phantom{0}} = 100$    f) $100 - \boxed{\phantom{0}} = 80$

**Challenge**

Draw lines to match the pairs of numbers that add up to 100.

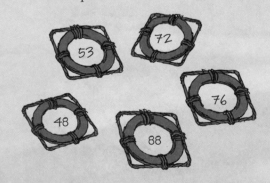

24   28   47   52   12   53   72   48   88   76

31

# Negative numbers

Any number that is greater than zero is a positive number. Numbers that are less than zero are called negative numbers. They are shown with a negative sign (-) in front of them. Positive numbers count forward from zero and negative numbers count backward from zero.

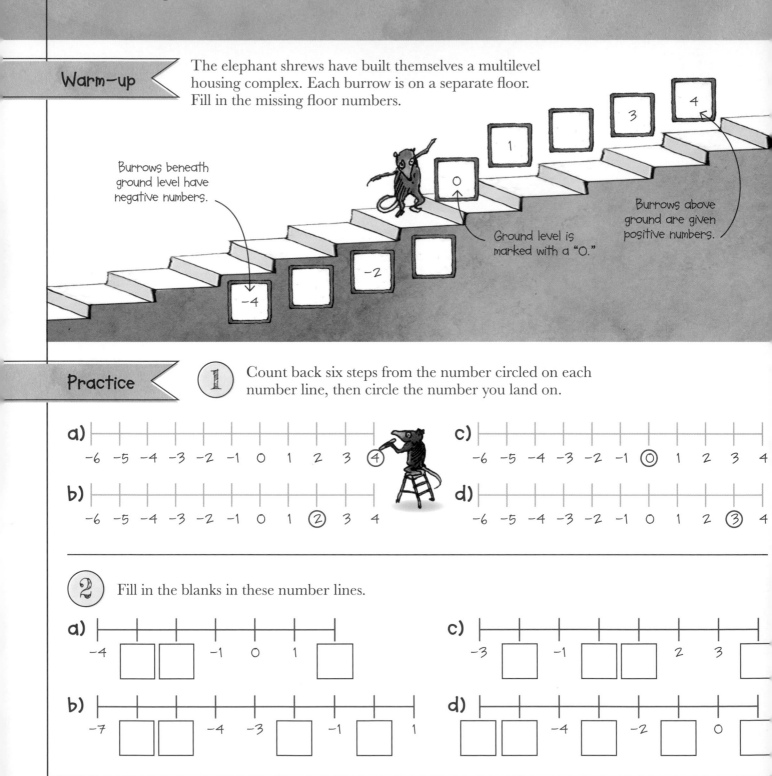

**Warm-up**

The elephant shrews have built themselves a multilevel housing complex. Each burrow is on a separate floor. Fill in the missing floor numbers.

Burrows beneath ground level have negative numbers.

Ground level is marked with a "O."

Burrows above ground are given positive numbers.

4

3

1

0

-2

-4

**Practice**

1) Count back six steps from the number circled on each number line, then circle the number you land on.

a)
-6  -5  -4  -3  -2  -1  0  1  2  3  ④

b)
-6  -5  -4  -3  -2  -1  0  1  ②  3  4

c)
-6  -5  -4  -3  -2  -1  ⓪  1  2  3  4

d)
-6  -5  -4  -3  -2  -1  0  1  2  ③  4

2) Fill in the blanks in these number lines.

a)
-4  ☐  ☐  -1  0  1  ☐

b)
-7  ☐  ☐  -4  -3  ☐  -1  ☐  1

c)
-3  ☐  -1  ☐  ☐  2  3  ☐

d)
☐  ☐  -4  ☐  -2  ☐  0

## Using a number line

We can use a number line to help add and subtract negative numbers. When you add a negative number, you move to the left, and when you subtract a negative number, you move to the right.

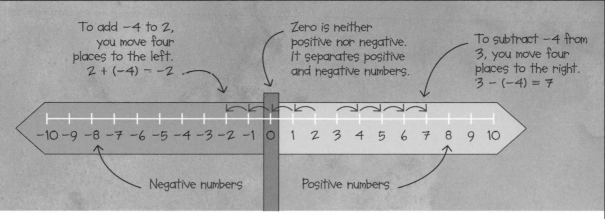

To add −4 to 2, you move four places to the left.
2 + (−4) = −2

Zero is neither positive nor negative. It separates positive and negative numbers.

To subtract −4 from 3, you move four places to the right.
3 − (−4) = 7

Negative numbers          Positive numbers

**3** Use the number lines to help you work out the difference between each pair of numbers.

**a)** −4 and 1 ▢

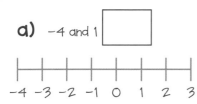

−4 −3 −2 −1 0 1 2 3

**b)** 1 and −5 ▢

−7 −6 −5 −4 −3 −2 −1 0 1

**c)** −8 and −4 ▢

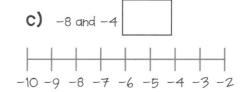

−10 −9 −8 −7 −6 −5 −4 −3 −2

**4** Use the elevator buttons to help you work out these number sentences.

**a)** (−1) + 3 = ▢

**c)** 4 + (−3) = ▢

**b)** (−1) − 3 = ▢

**d)** (−2) − (−2) = ▢

−4 −3 −2 −1 0 1 2 3 4

**5** Put these numbers in order of size. Start with the smallest.

−5   1   −8   −3   −7

▢ ▢ ▢ ▢ ▢

Challenge

In winter, the lowest temperature in a town is -15°F. In summer, the highest temperature in the same place is 75°F. What is the difference between the two temperatures?

(−15) + 75 = ▢ °F

33

# Multiplication

Multiplication is an easy way of adding one number lots of times. When we write "4 x 5," it means the same as "5 + 5 + 5 + 5" or "4 groups of 5." The cross symbol (x) means "multiply by," or "times."

Warm-up During their artistic swimming routine, a team of 15 mammoths organize themselves into smaller groups.

First, they organize themselves into groups of 5, so 15 = 5 + 5 + 5, or 5 × 3.

Then they organize themselves into groups of 3, so 3 + 3 + 3 + 3 + 3, or 3 × 5.

This shows that it doesn't matter which way around you multiply two numbers—the answer will be the same.

**5 x 3 = 15**

**3 x 5 = 15**

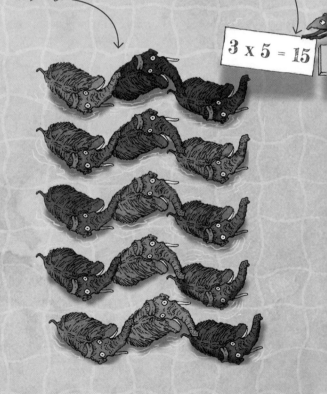

There are 12 mammoths on another swimming team. Fill in the blanks to show how they could arrange themselves into different groups.

a) ☐ × 12 = 12

b) ☐ × 1 = 12

c) ☐ × 6 = 12

d) ☐ × 2 = 12

e) ☐ × 4 = 12

f) ☐ × 3 = 12

## Multiplying using times tables

A "times table" is a list of multiplications. It is a good idea to memorize your times tables up to 12.

The "one times table" is a list of the multiplications of groups of 1.

The "two times table" is a list of the multiplications of groups of 2.

The numbers being multiplied are called factors.

$$2 \times 1 = 2$$
$$2 \times 2 = 4$$

$$1 \times 1 = 1$$
$$1 \times 2 = 2$$

The result of a multiplication is called the product.

## Multiplying using arrays

You can use arrays to help you with multiplication. An array shows items or shapes arranged in rows and columns.

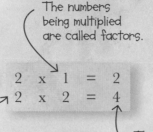

$5 \times 2 = 10$

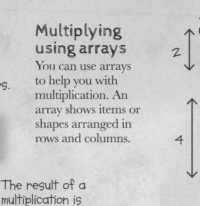

$5 \times 4 = 20$

## Practice

**1)** Write the number of mammoths as an addition sentence and as a multiplication sentence.

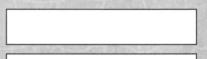

**2)** Write the number of swim rings as an addition sentence and as a multiplication sentence.

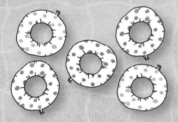

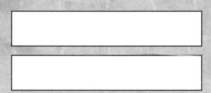

**3)** Write the number of elephant shrews as an addition sentence and as a multiplication sentence.

**4)** Write the number of beach balls as an addition sentence and as a multiplication sentence.

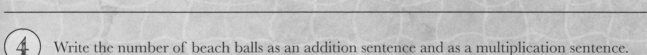

35

**5** Write the number of pairs of swimming goggles as an addition sentence and as a multiplication sentence.

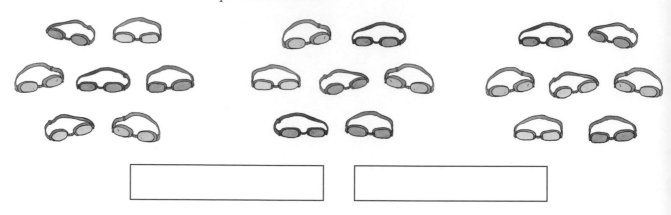

[ ] [ ]

**6** Use the number lines to work out these multiplication sentences. The first one has been done for you.

a)
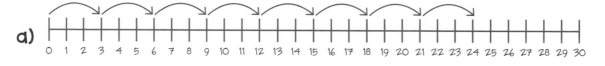
$3 \times 8 =$ [24]

b)

$4 \times 7 =$ [ ]

c)

$6 \times 5 =$ [ ]

**7** Use the number line to solve these problems.

a) The shrews buy 5 packs of pens. There are 5 pens in each pack. How many pens are there in total?

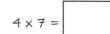 [ ] × [ ] = [ ]

b) The shrews buy 9 packs of erasers. There are 4 erasers in each pack. How many erasers are there in total?

[ ] × [ ] = [ ]

c) The mammoths have 2 boxes with 6 balls inside. They are given 2 more boxes of 6 balls. How many balls do they have in total?

[ ] × [ ] = [ ]

**8** Draw lines to match each multiplication with the correct answer.

a) 3 × 9    b) 11 × 4    c) 8 × 9    d) 10 × 3

44    27    30    35    8    64    60    72

e) 4 × 2    f) 5 × 7    g) 8 × 8    h) 12 × 5

**9** Circle the correct answer to each multiplication calculation.

a) 13 × 0    13    0    12

b) 10 × 7    168    69    70

c) 2 × 10    210    20    200

d) 2 × 8    17    16    32

e) 4 × 4    16    17    18

f) 4 × 12    46    47    48

g) 6 × 11    65    66    68

**10** Fill in the missing numbers in this multiplication grid.

| ×  | 1  | 2  | 3  | 4  | 5  | 6  | 7  | 8  | 9  | 10  | 11 | 12  |
|----|----|----|----|----|----|----|----|----|----|-----|----|-----|
| 1  | 1  | 2  | 3  | 4  | 5  | 6  | 7  |    |    |     | 11 |     |
| 2  | 2  |    | 6  |    |    | 12 | 14 | 16 |    |     | 22 | 24  |
| 3  | 3  | 6  | 9  |    |    | 18 |    | 24 |    | 30  |    | 36  |
| 4  |    | 8  |    | 16 | 20 |    | 28 |    | 36 |     | 44 |     |
| 5  | 5  |    | 15 |    |    | 30 | 35 |    | 45 |     | 55 |     |
| 6  |    | 12 | 18 |    |    | 36 | 42 |    | 54 | 60  |    | 72  |
| 7  | 7  |    | 21 | 28 |    |    | 49 | 56 |    |     |    | 84  |
| 8  | 8  | 16 |    |    | 40 | 48 |    |    | 72 | 80  |    | 96  |
| 9  |    | 18 |    |    | 45 |    | 63 | 72 |    |     | 99 | 108 |
| 10 |    |    | 30 | 40 |    | 60 |    |    |    | 100 |    |     |
| 11 | 11 | 22 |    | 44 |    |    | 77 | 88 |    |     |    | 132 |
| 12 | 12 |    | 36 |    | 60 | 72 |    |    | 108|     |    |     |

**Challenge**

The elephant shrews have 8 packets of 4 candies.
The mammoth has 4 packets of 9 candies.
Who has the greatest number of candies?

_____

37

# Division

We use the term "division" in math to describe splitting or sharing out a number or amount into smaller equal amounts. Division is the inverse, or opposite, of multiplication. We can use division to discover how many times one number fits into another.

**Warm-up**

When the 15 swimming mammoths split into groups of 3, they form 5 groups.

**a)** If they divided into groups of 5 instead, how many groups would there be? ☐

**b)** Could the mammoths divide into two equal groups? Circle the correct answer.

Yes     No

**Practice**

① Use the swimming mammoths to work out the answers to these calculations.

**a)** What is 10 ÷ 2? ☐    **b)** What is 9 ÷ 3? ☐    **c)** What is 14 ÷ 2? ☐

## Dividing equally

If we have 12 beach balls and we want to split them into 3 groups of 4, we write this as 12 ÷ 3 = 4.

## Division number sentences

Division number sentences use the "÷" symbol, which means "divide by." Each number in the sentence has its own name, too.

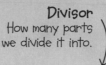

**Divisor** How many parts we divide it into.

**Quotient** How much is in each part.

$$12 \div 4 = 3$$

**Dividend** The number we divide.

---

**2** Use the beach balls to work out the answers to the number sentences. Draw circles around the beach balls to group them into twos, then count the number of groups. The first one has been done for you.

**a)**   4 grouped in 2s = ⟨ 2 ⟩ groups  so  4 ÷ 2 = ⟨ 2 ⟩

**b)**   6 grouped in 2s = ⟨   ⟩ groups  so  6 ÷ 2 = ⟨   ⟩

**c)**   12 grouped in 2s = ⟨   ⟩ groups  so  12 ÷ 2 = ⟨   ⟩

---

**3** Use the beach balls to work out the answers to the number sentences. Draw circles around the beach balls to group them into twos, then count the number of groups.

**a)** What is 16 ÷ 2? ⟨   ⟩

**b)** What is 8 ÷ 2? ⟨   ⟩

**c)** What is 18 ÷ 2? ⟨   ⟩

---

**4** Draw lines to match the number sentences with the correct answers.

36 ÷ 9    48 ÷ 8    21 ÷ 7    48 ÷ 6    6 ÷ 6

4 ÷ 2    18 ÷ 2    28 ÷ 4    30 ÷ 6

 8   1   5   4   2   6   3   7   9

39

**5** Divide the apples between the elephant shrews. Remember to include the remainder in your answers. The first one has been done for you.

**a)** $14 \div 3 =$ | **4 r2** | **c)** $11 \div 4 =$ | | **e)** $13 \div 5 =$ | |

> Some numbers cannot be divided into equal groups. For example, if there are 13 apples, then there will be 3 groups of 4 and 1 spare. The one that is left over is called the remainder. You write this as: $13 \div 4 = 3$ r1.

**b)** $15 \div 2 =$ | | **d)** $9 \div 3 =$ | | **f)** $15 \div 5 =$ | |

---

**6** Use the multiplication square to match up the answers to these number sentences. The first one has been done for you.

**a)** $24 \div 8 =$    5

**b)** $28 \div 7 =$    3

**c)** $25 \div 5 =$    3

**d)** $27 \div 9 =$    4

> To work out the answer to $24 \div 8$, choose the column with 8 at the top, then move down until you find 24. Then read across to find the answer, 3.

| X | 1 | 2 | 3 | 4 | 5 | 6 | 7 | 8 | 9 | 10 | 11 | 12 |
|---|---|---|---|---|---|---|---|---|---|----|----|----|
| 1 | 1 | 2 | 3 | 4 | 5 | 6 | 7 | 8 | 9 | 10 | 11 | 12 |
| 2 | 2 | 4 | 6 | 8 | 10 | 12 | 14 | 16 | 18 | 20 | 22 | 24 |
| 3 | 3 | 6 | 9 | 12 | 15 | 18 | 21 | 24 | 27 | 30 | 33 | 36 |
| 4 | 4 | 8 | 12 | 16 | 20 | 24 | 28 | 32 | 36 | 40 | 44 | 48 |
| 5 | 5 | 10 | 15 | 20 | 25 | 30 | 35 | 40 | 45 | 50 | 55 | 60 |
| 6 | 6 | 12 | 18 | 24 | 30 | 36 | 42 | 48 | 54 | 60 | 66 | 72 |
| 7 | 7 | 14 | 21 | 28 | 35 | 42 | 49 | 56 | 63 | 70 | 77 | 84 |
| 8 | 8 | 16 | 24 | 32 | 40 | 48 | 56 | 64 | 72 | 80 | 88 | 96 |
| 9 | 9 | 18 | 27 | 36 | 45 | 54 | 63 | 72 | 81 | 90 | 99 | 108 |
| 10 | 10 | 20 | 30 | 40 | 50 | 60 | 70 | 80 | 90 | 100 | 110 | 120 |
| 11 | 11 | 22 | 33 | 44 | 55 | 66 | 77 | 88 | 99 | 110 | 121 | 132 |
| 12 | 12 | 24 | 36 | 48 | 60 | 72 | 84 | 96 | 108 | 120 | 132 | 144 |

**7** Use the multiplication square to find the answers to these number sentences.

a) 32 ÷ 8 = ☐

b) 35 ÷ 7 = ☐

c) 30 ÷ 5 = ☐

d) 36 ÷ 9 = ☐

e) 42 ÷ 6 = ☐

f) 45 ÷ 9 = ☐

g) 40 ÷ 5 = ☐

h) 48 ÷ 6 = ☐

i) 24 ÷ 12 = ☐

**8** Complete these number sentences to show that division is the inverse of multiplication.

a) 6 × 9 = ☐

54 ÷ 6 = ☐

b) 7 × 8 = ☐

56 ÷ 8 = ☐

c) 10 × 5 = ☐

50 ÷ 5 = ☐

d) 10 × 6 = ☐

60 ÷ 6 = ☐

e) 8 × 8 = ☐

64 ÷ 8 = ☐

f) 7 × 9 = ☐

63 ÷ 7 = ☐

g) 8 × 9 = ☐

72 ÷ 8 = ☐

h) 9 × 9 = ☐

81 ÷ 9 = ☐

i) 4 × 7 = ☐

28 ÷ 4 = ☐

**Challenge**

The elephant shrew swimming club needs to order 30 new pairs of goggles and 20 new swim rings.

The pairs of goggles come in packs of four.

a) How many packs do they need to buy? ☐

b) Will there be any spares? ☐

The swim rings come in packs of two.

c) How many packs do they need to buy? ☐

d) Will there be any spares? ☐

# Factors

If we divide a number into exact equal parts, we find its factors. A factor is a whole number that can divide exactly into another number. Every number has at least two factors because a number can be divided by 1 and itself.

**Finding factors**
To find the factors of a number, we divide it into equal groups. Factors always come in pairs. The number 6 has the factor pairs 1 and 6 as well as 2 and 3. The factors of 6 are therefore 1, 2, 3, and 6.

**Warm-up**

The elephant shrews are investigating factors of 8 using their swamp-grass muffins.

They have arranged the muffins in different ways. What are the factors they have found? Help them work it out by filling in the blanks.

\_\_\_\_\_ group of \_\_\_\_\_ muffins           \_\_\_\_\_ groups of \_\_\_\_\_ muffins

The shrews have found that the factors of 8 are \_\_\_\_\_, \_\_\_\_\_, \_\_\_\_\_, and \_\_\_\_\_.

**Practice**

**1** Fill in the factor pairs for these numbers. The first one has been done for you.

a) 15    $1 \times 15 = 15$    $3 \times 5 = 15$

b) 26    $\boxed{\phantom{0}} \times \boxed{\phantom{0}} = 26$    $\boxed{\phantom{0}} \times \boxed{\phantom{0}} = 26$

c) 12    $\boxed{\phantom{0}} \times \boxed{\phantom{0}} = 12$    $\boxed{\phantom{0}} \times \boxed{\phantom{0}} = 12$    $\boxed{\phantom{0}} \times \boxed{\phantom{0}} = 12$

d) 32    $\boxed{\phantom{0}} \times \boxed{\phantom{0}} = 32$    $\boxed{\phantom{0}} \times \boxed{\phantom{0}} = 32$    $\boxed{\phantom{0}} \times \boxed{\phantom{0}} = 32$

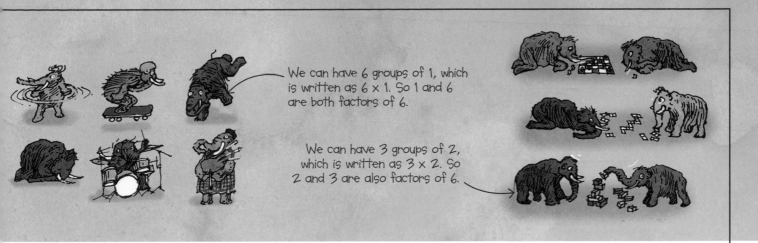

We can have 6 groups of 1, which is written as 6 × 1. So 1 and 6 are both factors of 6.

We can have 3 groups of 2, which is written as 3 × 2. So 2 and 3 are also factors of 6.

② The elephant shrews have discovered a family of factor bugs living nearby. Each bug shows the factors for a number. Fill in the circles with the factors for each of the numbers given. The first one has been done for you.

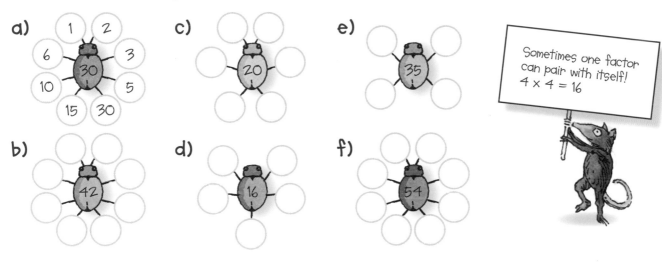

a) 1 2 6 3 10 5 15 30 — 30

c) — 20

e) — 35

Sometimes one factor can pair with itself!
4 × 4 = 16

b) — 42

d) — 16

f) — 54

③ Draw a circle around the elephant shrews that show the common factors of 48 and 64.

1   3   6   12   24   2   4   8   16   32

Challenge

What is the highest common factor for these pairs of numbers?

a) 48 and 64 ☐    c) 24 and 60 ☐

b) 30 and 48 ☐    d) 16 and 24 ☐

# Prime numbers

A prime number is a whole number bigger than 1 that can only be divided by itself and 1. Number 1 is not a prime number. To know whether a number is a prime, you should check whether it can be divided by 2, 3, 5, or 7.

## Warm-up

The elephant shrews are helping the mammoths package up the special prime numbers. Write in three more prime numbers under 10 for the shrews to wrap up.

The number 2 is the only even prime number. All the others are odd numbers.

## Practice

1. Color in the houses that have prime numbers.

2. Circle the prime numbers in each set.

a) 2    16    20    60    37

b) 26    62    53    81    73

c) 6    41    42    22    66

d) 61    60    79    92    102

## Factor trees

Prime numbers are the building blocks for all other numbers. We can show this using a factor tree.

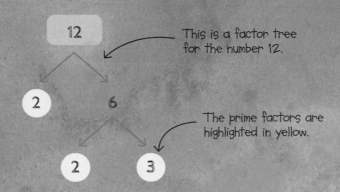

This is a factor tree for the number 12.

The prime factors are highlighted in yellow.

Any number that can be divided by 2, 3, 5, or 7 has more than two factors and can't be a prime.

**3** Look at these sequences of numbers. Circle the sequences that are prime number sequences.

a) 12, 18, 24, 30, 36, 42

b) 13, 17, 19, 23, 29, 31

c) 2, 3, 5, 7, 11, 13

d) 33, 35, 37, 39, 50, 55

e) 83, 79, 73, 71, 67, 61

f) 107, 105, 103, 101, 97

**4** Fill in the missing factors for each of these factor trees. Make sure all the branches end with prime numbers. The first one has been done for you.

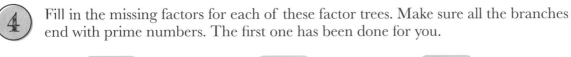

a) 30
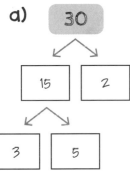
15   2
3   5

b) 42
[ ]   2
[ ]   [ ]

c) 24
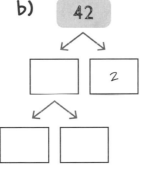
[ ]   2
6   [ ]
[ ]   [ ]

d) 36
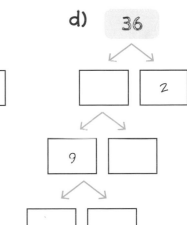
[ ]   2
9   [ ]
[ ]   [ ]

### Challenge

One of the elephant shrews has forgotten the combination to the suitcase. The code is the ones digit of the fifth, sixth, seventh, and eighth prime numbers, written from the smallest to the largest.

Can you fill in the combination?

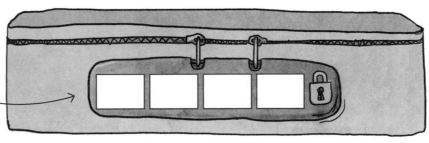

45

# Square numbers

When you multiply a whole number by itself, the result is called a square number. They are called square numbers because you can show each number as an actual square.

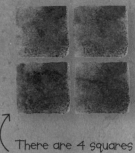

There are 4 squares here, so $2^2 = 4$.

Warm-up

The elephant shrews are using blocks to print a sequence of larger and larger square numbers. Help them find the value of each of these square numbers by counting the printed squares. Fill in the square numbers in the boxes below.

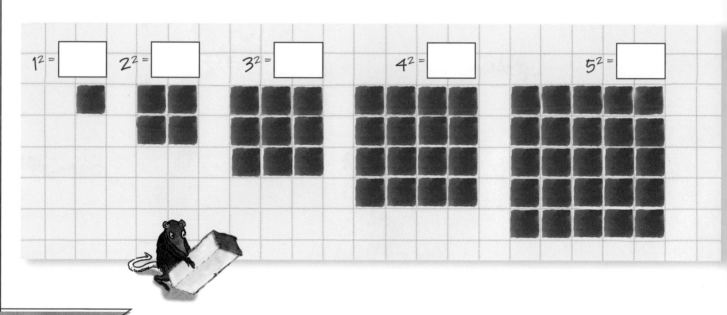

$1^2 =$ [ ]    $2^2 =$ [ ]    $3^2 =$ [ ]    $4^2 =$ [ ]    $5^2 =$ [ ]

Practice

**1** Color in squares on this grid to show the square number $6^2$.

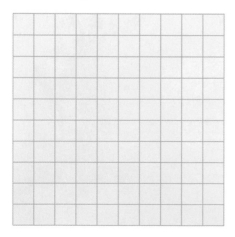

**2** Write these as square numbers. The first one has been done for you.

a) $12 \times 12$    $\boxed{12^2}$    e) $8 \times 8$    [ ]

b) $15 \times 15$    [ ]    f) $91 \times 91$    [ ]

c) $36 \times 36$    [ ]

d) $67 \times 67$    [ ]

## Showing square numbers

Two rows of blue squares represent 2 x 2 or 2 squared. We write square numbers like this:

$2^2$

The small 2 means squared.

## Square roots

The number that you multiply by itself to find a square number is known as that number's square root. All square numbers have square roots. Square numbers and square roots are inverse operations of each other.

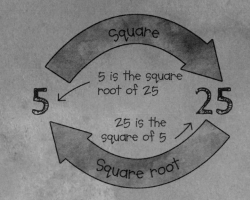

Square

5 is the square root of 25

5     25

25 is the square of 5

Square root

---

 **3** Shade the square numbers from $7^2$ to $10^2$ on this grid. The first one has been done for you.

| 41 | 42 | 43 | 44 | 45 | 46 | 47 | 48 | 49 | 50 |
|----|----|----|----|----|----|----|----|----|----|
| 51 | 52 | 53 | 54 | 55 | 56 | 57 | 58 | 59 | 60 |
| 61 | 62 | 63 | 64 | 65 | 66 | 67 | 68 | 69 | 70 |
| 71 | 72 | 73 | 74 | 75 | 76 | 77 | 78 | 79 | 80 |
| 81 | 82 | 83 | 84 | 85 | 86 | 87 | 88 | 89 | 90 |
| 91 | 92 | 93 | 94 | 95 | 96 | 97 | 98 | 99 | 100 |

**4** Circle the number below that is not a square number.

49          52

64

81          100

---

**5** Draw lines to match the square numbers to the square roots.

Square numbers

 9     16     25     4

Square roots

 5     3     2     4

---

 Challenge

Write the square roots for these numbers.

a) 49 ☐     c) 81 ☐     e) 121 ☐

b) 36 ☐     d) 64 ☐     f) 100 ☐

The symbol for a square root is √.

47

# Cube numbers

A cube number gets its name because it can be shown as a cube shape. It is a whole number that is multiplied by itself, then by itself again. Cube numbers are written with a small 3, like this: $2^3$.

**Warm-up**

The mammoths like a lot of sugar in their coffee! Help the elephant shrews work out how many sugar cubes they have stacked up ready for the mammoths. Write the missing cube numbers in the boxes. The first one has been done for you.

The shrew is still working hard to build this cube! When it is completed, it will be 4 x 4 x 4.

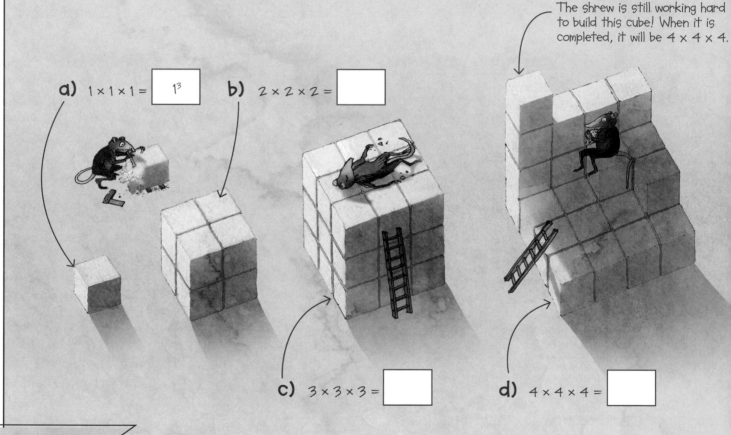

a) $1 \times 1 \times 1 = \boxed{1^3}$    b) $2 \times 2 \times 2 = \boxed{\phantom{0}}$

c) $3 \times 3 \times 3 = \boxed{\phantom{0}}$    d) $4 \times 4 \times 4 = \boxed{\phantom{0}}$

## Practice

**1** Write these as cube numbers using a small 3.

a) $8 \times 8 \times 8$ $\boxed{\phantom{0}}$    c) $51 \times 51 \times 51$ $\boxed{\phantom{0}}$

b) $13 \times 13 \times 13$ $\boxed{\phantom{0}}$    d) $99 \times 99 \times 99$ $\boxed{\phantom{0}}$

## Cube shapes

The first cube number is one cube long, one cube high, and one cube deep. The next cube number is two cubes long, two cubes high, and two cubes deep.

$1 \times 1 \times 1 = 1$ or $1^3$

$2 \times 2 \times 2 = 8$ or $2^3$

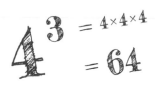

The small 3 we use for a cube number is called an exponent or power. So we can say that in the cube number $4^3$, the number 4 has been multiplied to the power of 3.

$4^3 = 4 \times 4 \times 4 = 64$

**(2)** Circle the picture that shows the cube number $2^3$.

**a)**

**b)**

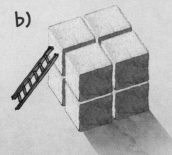

**c)**

**(3)** Which of these is a cube number?

 9      25      27      36

You could use cubes to build the shapes to help you.

**(4)** How many sugar cubes will an elephant shrew need to build these shapes?

**a)** A cube with 5 sides each. ☐

**b)** A cube with 6 sides each. ☐

**(5)** Write all of the cube numbers up to 100. ☐

 **Challenge** Which cube number, less than 100, is also a square number?

☐

# Magic shapes

Numbers and shapes can be combined to create clever number puzzles called magic shapes.

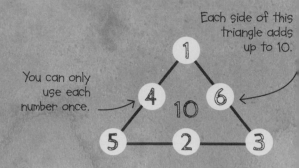

Each side of this triangle adds up to 10.

You can only use each number once.

The elephant shrews have been digging holes to create a magic triangle game. They are now trying to work out which number goes in each hole so that each side adds up to the magic number 20. Each number from 1–9 should appear once in the magic triangle. Write the missing numbers on the correct balls.

Magic number: 20

20

Use the following numbers:
1, 2, 3, 4, 5, 6, 7, 8, 9

50

# Magic triangles

In a magic triangle, the numbers on each side of the triangle must add up to the magic number in the middle.

Each row adds up to 34.

Both diagonals add up to 34.

| 16 | 3 | 2 | 13 |
|----|----|----|----|
| 5 | 10 | 11 | 8 |
| 9 | 6 | 7 | 12 |
| 4 | 15 | 14 | 1 |

Each column adds up to 34.

The four numbers in the corners also add up to 34.

# Magic squares

In a magic square, every column, row, and diagonal line adds up to the same magic number. The numbers in the four corners also add up to the same number.

## Practice

**1** Solve these magic triangles.

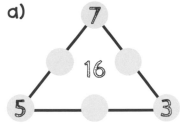

a) 7, 16, 5, 3

b) 11, 28, 9, 7

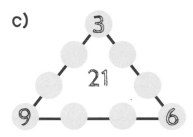
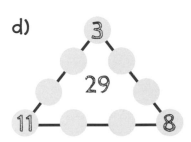
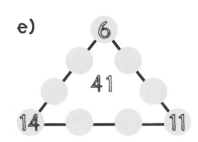

c) 3, 21, 9, 6

d) 3, 29, 11, 8

e) 6, 41, 14, 11

**2** Use the numbers given to solve this magic square. The magic number is 46.

 5

 8

9

4

| 19 | 6 |  | 16 |
|----|----|----|----|
|  | 13 | 14 | 11 |
| 12 |  | 10 | 15 |
| 7 | 18 | 17 |  |

**3** The elephant shrews have nearly finished this magic square where the magic number is 42. Help them finish the puzzle.

| 4 |  | 14 | 15 |
|----|----|----|----|
| 18 | 11 |  | 5 |
| 7 | 6 | 17 |  |
|  | 16 | 3 | 10 |

**Challenge**

Solve this magic square.

7   9   25

| 27 |  | 5 | 33 |
|----|----|----|----|
| 17 | 21 | 23 | 11 |
|  | 13 | 15 | 19 |
| 3 | 31 | 29 |  |

Magic number = ☐

# Equations

An equation is a number sentence that contains an equals sign (=). This sign means "is the same as" and shows that whatever is on one side of it has exactly the same value as what is on the other side. For example, 3 × 6 = 18.

Warm-up

The mammoths are trying to show the elephant shrews how equations need to balance using a see-saw. Fill in the blanks using the words in the box to make sure they have explained it correctly.

equals    balanced    4    same

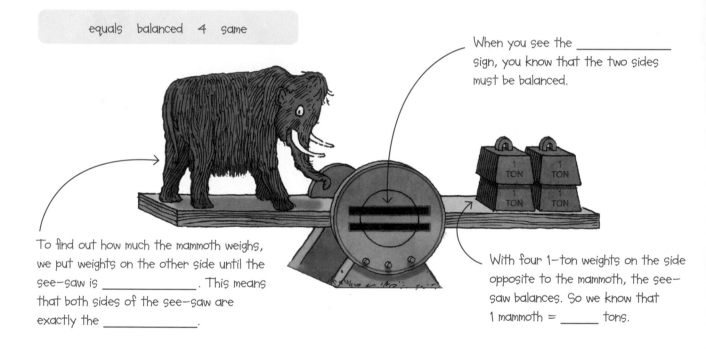

When you see the _____ sign, you know that the two sides must be balanced.

To find out how much the mammoth weighs, we put weights on the other side until the see-saw is _____. This means that both sides of the see-saw are exactly the _____.

With four 1-ton weights on the side opposite to the mammoth, the see-saw balances. So we know that 1 mammoth = _____ tons.

Practice

1. How many shrews need to be added to the left-hand side of the see-saw for it to be balanced?

## Algebra

You can use the fact that both sides of an equation must be the same to find values that you don't yet know. In math, we often use a letter for the value we don't know. This is called algebra.

$3 \times 6$ is 18. So to make both sides of the equation the same, "a" must be 18.

$$a \stackrel{=}{\bigcirc} 3 \times 6$$

To find the value of "b," we can rearrange the equation. As long as we do the same thing to each side, the equation will still balance.

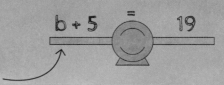
$$b + 5 \stackrel{=}{\bigcirc} 19$$

We can take 5 away from each side to give b = 19 − 5. So "b" = 14.

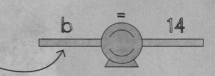
$$b \stackrel{=}{\bigcirc} 14$$

---

**2** Find the missing numbers in these number sentences.

**a)** $3 + \boxed{\phantom{0}} = 12$

**b)** $5 + \boxed{\phantom{0}} = 21$

**c)** $7 + \boxed{\phantom{0}} = 25$

**d)** $14 - \boxed{\phantom{0}} = 9$

**e)** $33 - \boxed{\phantom{0}} = 12$

**f)** $58 - \boxed{\phantom{0}} = 21$

---

**3** Find the missing numbers in these number sentences.

**a)** $4 \times \boxed{\phantom{0}} = 16$

**b)** $7 \times \boxed{\phantom{0}} = 21$

**c)** $8 \times \boxed{\phantom{0}} = 40$

**d)** $20 \times \boxed{\phantom{0}} = 80$

**e)** $30 \times \boxed{\phantom{0}} = 60$

**f)** $45 \times \boxed{\phantom{0}} = 180$

---

**4** Find the value of the letters in these number sentences.

**a)** $a + 7 = 28$    $a = \boxed{\phantom{0}}$

**b)** $b + 12 = 47$    $b = \boxed{\phantom{0}}$

**c)** $c - 8 = 51$    $c = \boxed{\phantom{0}}$

**d)** $d - 13 = 64$    $d = \boxed{\phantom{0}}$

---

**Challenge**

Find the value of the letters in these number sentences.

**a)** $3 \times 5 = 4 + a$    $a = \boxed{\phantom{0}}$

**b)** $6 \times 7 = 38 + b$    $b = \boxed{\phantom{0}}$

**c)** $9 \times 9 = 73 + c$    $c = \boxed{\phantom{0}}$

**d)** $4 \times 9 = 26 + d$    $d = \boxed{\phantom{0}}$

# Fractions

A fraction is part of a whole. It can either be a smaller part of one thing, like a pie cut into slices, or part of a group, like half the mammoths in a group.

**Warm-up**

The mammoths have been baking swamp-grass pies for the elephant shrews. Can you help the mammoths work out what fraction of each pie has been eaten? Write the fraction in the box below. The first one has been done for you.

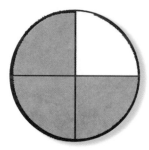  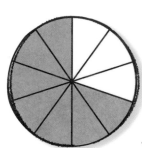

a) $\boxed{1/4}$  b) $\boxed{\phantom{0}}$  c) $\boxed{\phantom{0}}$

**Practice**

**1** Draw lines to match the pink slices of pie with the written fractions.

a) 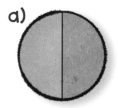  b) 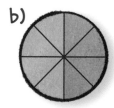  c) 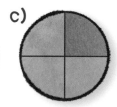  d) 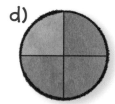  e) 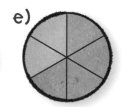  f)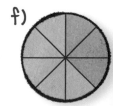

 $\dfrac{1}{4}$    $\dfrac{3}{4}$   $\dfrac{1}{2}$    $\dfrac{3}{8}$    $\dfrac{4}{6}$    $\dfrac{4}{8}$

54

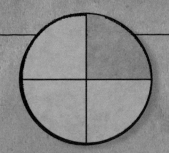

### Fraction of a whole
This pie has been cut into 4 equal parts, but ¼ has been shaded pink.

### Equivalent fractions
Fractions can be written in different ways. This pie has been cut into 8 equal parts, but ²⁄₈ has been shaded pink. This is the same amount as ¼. We call these equivalent fractions.

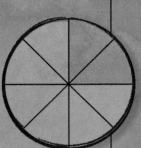

### Fraction of a group
There are 4 swamp-grass muffins here, but 1 of them, or ¼ of the group, has strawberry frosting.

**2** Draw and shade in the pies to match the fractions given below. The first one has been done for you.

a)
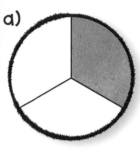
¹⁄₃

b)
¹⁄₄

c)
¹⁄₆

d)
²⁄₄

e)
³⁄₆

---

**3** What fraction of these groups of swamp-grass muffins have strawberry frosting? The first one has been done for you.

a)
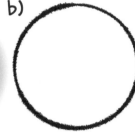
| ¹⁄₄ |

c)
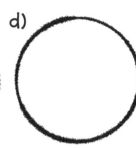
☐

e)
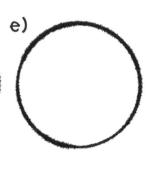
☐

b)

☐

d)
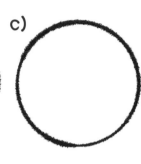
☐

f)

☐

Circle one third of each of these groups of swamp-grass muffins.

a)

b)

c)

5 For each pair of pies, write the fraction of pink slices in the box. Then circle the one with the bigger fraction of pink slices. The first one has been done for you.

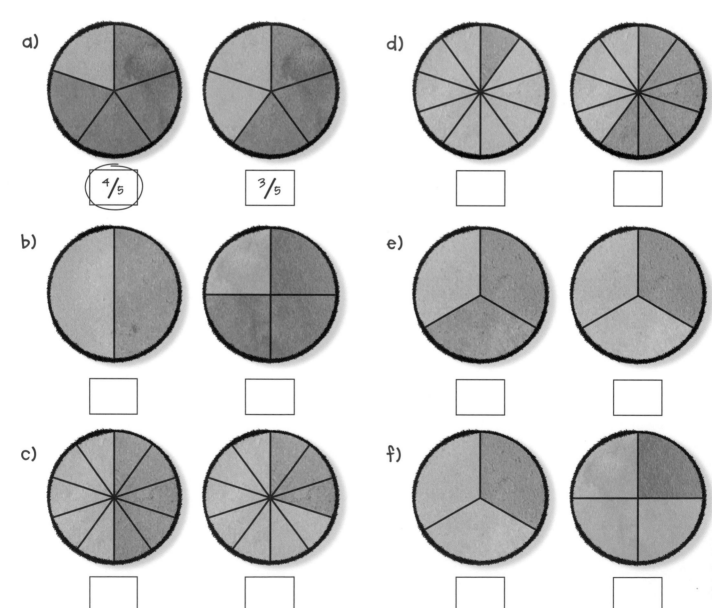

a)

$\frac{4}{5}$   $\frac{3}{5}$

b)

c)

d)

e)

f)

**6** These pies have been cut into a different number of slices, but some show the same amount of pie. Draw lines to match the pairs of equivalent fractions.

**7** Shade the blank pies to make pairs of equivalent fractions. Then write the fractions of pink slices underneath.

a)

1/2

[ ]

b)

2/6

[ ]

c)

2/8

[ ]

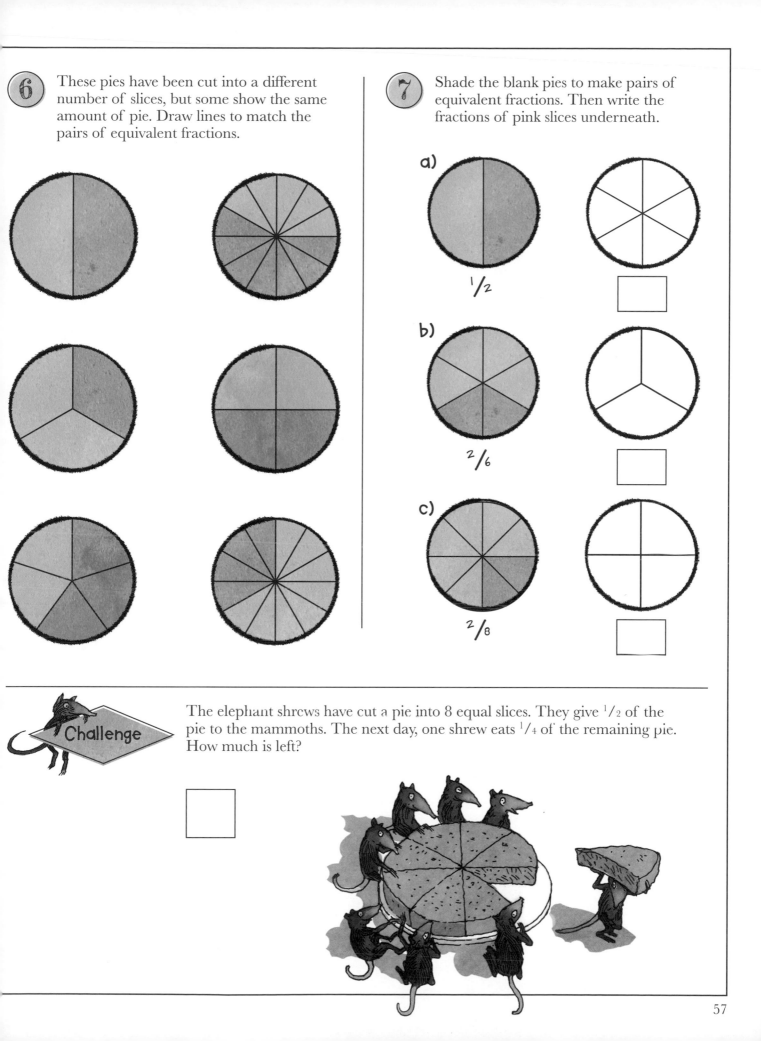

**Challenge**

The elephant shrews have cut a pie into 8 equal slices. They give 1/2 of the pie to the mammoths. The next day, one shrew eats 1/4 of the remaining pie. How much is left?

[ ]

57

# Improper fractions and mixed numbers

A proper fraction is where the number of parts are less than the whole (like $^1/_2$ or $^3/_5$). Sometimes, fractions are more than one whole (like $^5/_2$ or $^7/_5$). These are called improper fractions and can also be written as mixed numbers (like $2^1/_2$).

## Warm-up

The mammoths are explaining the different types of fractions to the elephant shrews. Draw lines to join these fractions with the correct category.

| Mixed number | Proper fraction | Improper fraction |
|---|---|---|

$^{11}/_3$     $6^4/_5$     $^{15}/_5$     $^3/_5$     $^2/_7$     $4^1/_3$     $^7/_2$

## Practice

**1** Write the improper fractions shown in these pictures. The first one has been done for you.

  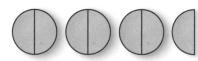 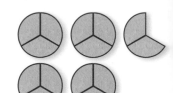

a) $^7/_5$     b) ☐     c) ☐     d) ☐

**2** This number line is divided into fifths.

**a)** Label $^8/_5$ and $^{17}/_5$ on the number line.

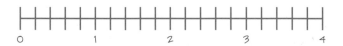

**b)** Write each fraction as a mixed number.

$^8/_5$ ☐     $^{17}/_5$ ☐

## Improper fractions

Improper fractions describe amounts that add up to more than one whole. Five halves can be written as:

 $\frac{5}{2}$ ← The numerator is bigger than the denominator.

## Mixed numbers

Mixed numbers are a different way of writing improper fractions. They have a whole number and a fraction.

The improper fraction $\frac{5}{2}$ is the same as the mixed number $2\frac{1}{2}$.

 $2\frac{1}{2}$

Whole number

Fraction

---

**3** Color in these shapes to show the mixed numbers.

a) $1\frac{1}{5}$    b) $2\frac{1}{2}$    c) $2\frac{3}{5}$    d) $2\frac{1}{3}$

---

**4** Draw lines to match each improper fraction with its mixed number partner.

$\frac{11}{2}$   $\frac{9}{2}$   $\frac{25}{4}$   $\frac{16}{5}$   $\frac{11}{3}$   $\frac{39}{4}$   $\frac{23}{3}$   $\frac{8}{5}$

$3\frac{2}{3}$   $7\frac{2}{3}$   $5\frac{1}{2}$   $6\frac{1}{4}$   $9\frac{3}{4}$   $1\frac{3}{5}$   $3\frac{1}{5}$   $4\frac{1}{2}$

---

**5** Change these numbers from an improper fraction to a mixed number.

a) $\frac{17}{3}$ ☐    b) $\frac{12}{5}$ ☐

**6** Change these numbers from a mixed number to an improper fraction.

a) $4\frac{1}{3}$ ☐    b) $2\frac{3}{8}$ ☐

---

 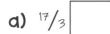 **Challenge**

The mammoths make some pies for the elephant shrews to share. Each shrew eats $\frac{1}{4}$ of a pie. In total they eat $6\frac{1}{4}$ pies.

How many shrews are there? ☐

# Decimals

Decimals are used to write parts (or fractions) of numbers. They show values between 0 and 1 or between two whole numbers. For example, 4.8 is a decimal that is greater than 4 but less than 5.

**Warm-up**

In the contest to grow the plumpest pumpkin, the mammoths aren't sure which pumpkin has won. The three finalists have masses of 4.04 kg, 4.99 kg, and 4.67 kg. Add the masses to the digital scales to put them in order from 3rd prize to 1st prize.

**Practice**

① Write the fractions of pink slices as decimals. The first one has been done for you.

a) [ 0.1 ]    b) [   ]    c) [   ]    d) [   ]    e) [   ]

60

The further a digit is to the right of the decimal point, the smaller the value it shows.

1.52 ←

Decimal point

**Fractions in disguise**

The numbers after the decimal point are another way of showing fractions.

The digit "8" is in the tenths column, so 0.8 is the same as $^8/_{10}$.

| Ones 1s | Tenths $^1/_{10}$ | Hundredths $^1/_{100}$ | Thousandths $^1/_{1000}$ |
|---|---|---|---|
| 0 . | 8 | 0 | 0 |

The digit "8" is in the hundredths column, so 0.08 is the same as $^8/_{100}$.

| Ones 1s | Tenths $^1/_{10}$ | Hundredths $^1/_{100}$ | Thousandths $^1/_{1000}$ |
|---|---|---|---|
| 0 . | 0 | 8 | 0 |

**2** The elephant shrews' vegetable garden has 100 plants of different kinds. Write the number of each type of plant as a decimal. The first one has been done for you.

a) The number of runner beans.        | 0.01 |

b) The number of cabbages.        | |

c) The number of carrots.        | |

d) The number of potatoes.        | |

**3** Write these decimals in order of size. Start with the smallest.

| 0.06 | 0.1 | 0.02 | 0.4 | 0.07 |

| | | | | |

**4** Ten mammoths went to a party. Three of them left early.

Write the number that stayed at the party as a decimal fraction of the original number at the party.        | |

**Challenge**

Draw lines to match the number to the correct description.

| 0.562 | 0.43 | 0.258 | 0.44 |

| The smallest number | The largest number | The tenths and hundredths digits are the same | The number has three hundredths |

# Percentages

Percent means out of 100.
Percentages are useful when you
are comparing different quantities.
The symbol "%" is used to show
a percentage.

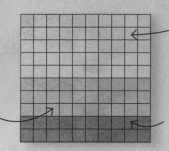

50 of the 100 squares are shaded green, so 50% of the shape is colored green.

30 of the 100 squares are shaded blue, so 30% of the shape is colored blue.

20 of the 100 squares are shaded purple, so 20% of the shape is colored purple.

Warm-up

One hundred elephant shrews have gathered to watch a mammoth blast off into space in a rocket.

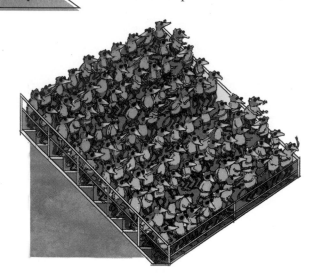

**a)** In the crowd of shrews, what percentage are wearing blue?

**b)** In the crowd of shrews, what percentage are wearing green?

**c)** In the crowd of shrews, what percentage are wearing yellow?

**d)** In the crowd of shrews, what percentage are not wearing blue or green?

**Practice**

**1** This picture shows 100 elephant shrews, 30 of which are colored purple. Follow the instructions.

**a)** Color 10% of the shrews blue.

**b)** Color 3% of the shrews green.

**c)** Color 6% of the shrews yellow.

**d)** What percentage are purple?

**e)** What percentage are colored in?

**f)** What percentage are not colored in?

62

## Working out percentages

We can find the percentage of any total amount. For example, this ladder is 12 m high and the elephant shrew has climbed up 6 m. To find the percentage of the ladder the shrew has climbed, first we need to work out the height that is 1% of 12 m by dividing by 100:

$$12 \text{ m} \div 100 = 0.12 \text{ m}$$

So 1% of 12 m is 0.12 m.

Then we divide the height the shrew has climbed by 0.12:

$$6 \text{ m} \div 0.12 \text{ m} = 50\%$$

The shrew has climbed 50% of the ladder.

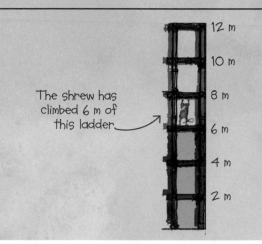

The shrew has climbed 6 m of this ladder.

12 m
10 m
8 m
6 m
4 m
2 m

---

**2** A mammoth has 100 ice cream cones to sell at the rocket launch. Of these, 14 are vanilla, 42 are chocolate, and the rest are blueberry.

What percentage of the ice cream cones are blueberry? ☐

14%   42%   ?

---

**3** What percentage of these shapes has been shaded a darker color?

a) ☐   b) ☐   c) ☐   d) ☐

---

Challenge

The mammoth's rocket is 20 m high. Can you work out what percentage of the rocket is formed by the nose cone, the middle section, and the tail? You'll need to work out the height of the middle section first.

Nose ☐

Middle ☐

Tail ☐

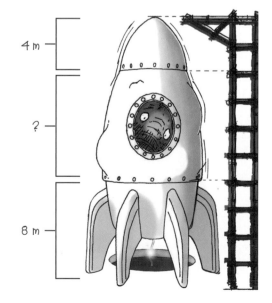

4 m

?

8 m

# Describing fractions

Decimals, fractions, and percentages are just different ways of showing the same value. This means that you can represent a fraction in different ways.

An elephant shrew has baked a swamp grass pie to share between friends. The shrew wants to convert the fractions of the pie into decimals and percentages. Fill in the blanks to help.

 1 whole = 100% = 1.00

 $^1/_{10} = {}^{10}/_{100} = 10\% = 0.1$

 $^1/_5 = \boxed{\phantom{0}}/_{10} = \boxed{\phantom{0}}/_{100} = \boxed{\phantom{0}}\% = 0.\boxed{\phantom{0}}$

 $^1/_2 = {}^5/_{10} = {}^{50}/_{100} = 50\% = 0.5$

 $^1/_4 = \boxed{\phantom{0}}/_{100} = \boxed{\phantom{0}}\% = 0.\boxed{\phantom{0}}$

---

**Practice**

**1** Shade the pies to show the fractions.

a) $^2/_{10}$   b) $^5/_{10}$   c) $^9/_{10}$   d) $^3/_{10}$   e) $^4/_{10}$

---

**2** Shade the pies to show the percentages.

a) 40%   b) 50%   c) 20%   d) 10%   e) 70%

## One number, three ways

Here is one-tenth shown as a decimal, a percentage, and a fraction.

Percentage

**10%**

Decimal — 0.10

Fraction → 1/10

---

**3** Shade the pies to show the decimals.

**a)** 0.6    **b)** 0.3    **c)** 0.8    **d)** 0.9    **e)** 0.5

---

**4** Complete this table.

| Fraction | Decimal | Percentage |
|----------|---------|------------|
| 1/10 |  | 10% |
| 1/2 | 0.5 |  |
| / | 0.2 | 20% |
| 1/4 | 0.25 |  |
| 3/4 |  | 75% |

**5** Draw lines to match each slice of pie with the correct number in the boxes below.

0.5    40%    0.8    6/10    7/10

| | | | | |
|---|---|---|---|---|
| 4/10 | 4/5 | 60% | 1/2 | 0.7 |

---

**6** Put these fractions, decimals, and percentages in order, with the smallest first.

3/4    0.2    10%    1/4    0.6    ☐ ☐ ☐ ☐ ☐

---

**Challenge**

Put these in order, with the smallest first.

☐ ☐ ☐ ☐ ☐

1.3    2 1/2    540%

0.7    4 3/4

# Ratio and proportion

Ratios are used to compare two numbers or quantities. They show how much bigger or smaller one amount is than another. We use the symbol ":" in ratios. A proportion compares part of an amount to the whole amount and can be written as a ratio, as a fraction, or a percentage.

Warm-up The elephant shrews are mixing up different shades of purple paint. What is the ratio of red paint to blue paint in each of these pictures?

a) ☐     b) ☐     c) ☐     d) ☐

Practice

**1** Draw lines to match each set of elephant shrews and mammoths with the correct ratio showing shrews to mammoths. The first one has been done for you.

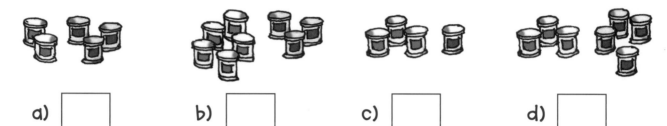

a)

b)

c)

d)

3:2

4:1

3:3

1:4

**2** Here are some cans of paint. Circle the correct proportion of each color.

a) Red     $\frac{4}{10}$     $\frac{3}{10}$          c) Blue     $\frac{1}{8}$     $\frac{1}{10}$

b) Green     $\frac{3}{8}$     $\frac{3}{10}$          d) Black     $\frac{2}{10}$     $\frac{2}{5}$

## Ratio

Ratios are written as two numbers to compare amounts.

  Here, there is one can of blue paint compared to three cans of red paint. There is three times more red than blue paint.

1:3

## Proportion

Proportion describes how much of the whole of something is taken up by a part of it. So if 30 cans of red paint and 10 cans of blue paint are mixed together, the whole contains (30 + 10 =) 40 cans of mixed-color paint. Then we can work out what proportion of the whole is red paint and what is blue paint.

Proportion of paint that is blue is $^{10}/_{40} = ^1/_4$

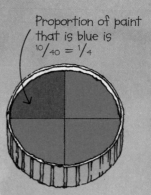

---

**3** The elephant shrews went bird watching. They saw 12 birds in one day. Write the proportion of each type of bird they saw as a fraction.

a)  = ☐

c)   = ☐

b)  = ☐

d)  = ☐

---

**4** A store had a total of 200 cans of paint in four different colors. Use the proportions given below to work out how many cans of each color were in the store. You can use a calculator to help you. The first one has been done for you.

a)  20%

b) 30%

c) 10%

d) 40%

a) | 20 | ÷ 100 = | 0.2 |

| 0.2 | × 200 = | 40 |

b) ☐ ÷ 100 = ☐

☐ × 200 = ☐

c) ☐ ÷ 100 = ☐

☐ × 200 = ☐

d) ☐ ÷ 100 = ☐

☐ × 200 = ☐

---

**Challenge**

The elephant shrews bought some new cans of paint. Complete the sentences to describe the cans.

a) For every 12 cans of red paint, there are ☐ cans of green paint.

b) For every 6 cans of red paint, there are ☐ cans of green paint.

c) For every 1 can of green paint, there are ☐ cans of red paint.

d) Compared to the total number of cans, the proportions are: green paint ☐ / ☐ red paint ☐ / ☐

67

# Scaling

Scaling is making something smaller or larger while keeping all its parts in proportion to each other. All parts are made bigger or smaller by the same amount.

## Map scales

Maps use ratio to show how much smaller the distances are on the map than they are in real life.

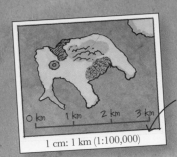

O km   1 km   2 km   3 km

1 cm: 1 km (1:100,000)

On this map, 1 cm represents 1 km.

Warm-up

A mammoth has made three different statues of an elephant shrew. Circle the statue that is a scale model of the shrew.

a)

b)

c)

Scale factor is the number that an object has been multiplied or divided by. The statue is two times larger than the shrew, so the scale factor is 2.

Practice

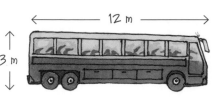

1.  Use the information to work out the scale factors for these statues. The first one has been done for you.

    a) Real height 25 cm        Statue height 50 cm        50 ÷ [ 25 ] = [ 2 ]

    b) Real height 300 cm       Statue height 100 cm       100 ÷ [   ] = [   ]

    c) Real height 25 cm        Statue height 150 cm       150 ÷ [   ] = [   ]

2.  The elephant shrews' bus is 12 m long and 3 m high. Models are made of the bus at different scales.

    ← 12 m →

    3 m

    a) Model 1 is 8 m long. What is the height?   Height = [   ] m

    b) Model 2 is half the size of model 1. What are the length and height?   Length = [   ] m   Height = [   ] m

68

## Scaling up

When we sculpt a statue, we may need to scale up the size of something small. For example, an elephant shrew is 25 cm tall in real life, but the statue is 100 cm tall.

Every part of the statue will be 4 times bigger than in real life, because 25 × 4 = 100. →

## Scaling down

When we take a photo, the image is a scaled-down version of the real thing. For example, the mammoth is 300 cm tall, but in the photo it's only 12 cm high.

Every part of the photo will be 25 times smaller than in real life, because 300 ÷ 12 = 25. →

---

 **3** The elephant shrews have a map that shows where the pumpkin patch is. Each 1 cm square on their map represents 10 m in real life. Work out these distances. The first one has been done for you.

**a)** The river island to the pumpkin patch is 3 cm on the map.

This is 3 × | 10 | m = | 30 | m in real life.

**b)** The swamp to the pumpkin patch is 8 cm on the map.

This is | | × | | m = | | m in real life.

**c)** The wood to the swamp is 6 cm on the map.

This is | | × | | m = | | m in real life.

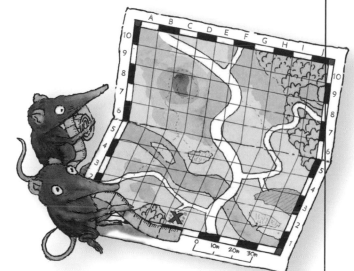

---

The elephant shrews have drawn a shape on the graph paper. Draw the same shape with a scale factor of 2.

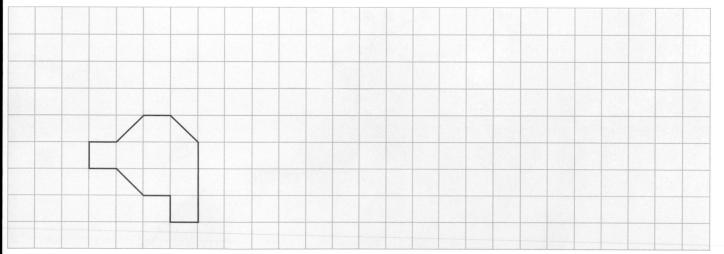

# Sequences

When we put numbers or shapes in a certain order, they make a sequence. Each number or shape in the sequence is called a term, and the set pattern that they follow is called a rule. A sequence can be based on addition, subtraction, multiplication, division, or a mixture of all four.

Warm-up

The elephant shrews have hung out clothes to dry in different sequences. Help them recognize the sequence rules by filling in the blanks with the correct information and adding numbers to the shirts.

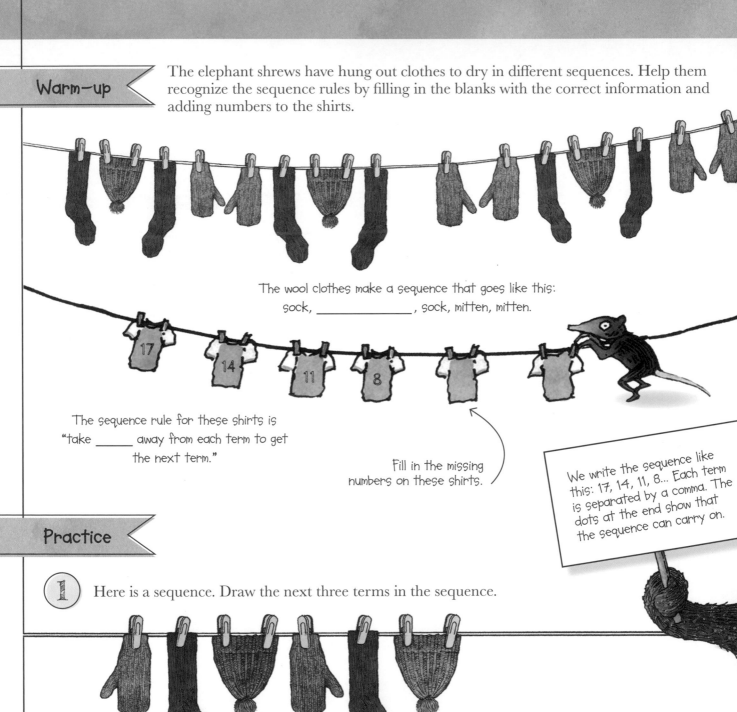

The wool clothes make a sequence that goes like this:
sock, _____, sock, mitten, mitten.

The sequence rule for these shirts is "take _____ away from each term to get the next term."

Fill in the missing numbers on these shirts.

We write the sequence like this: 17, 14, 11, 8... Each term is separated by a comma. The dots at the end show that the sequence can carry on.

Practice

(1) Here is a sequence. Draw the next three terms in the sequence.

## Sequence rules

A sequence rule can be used to find the next terms in the sequence. The first number in a sequence is called the first term. An unknown is called the "nth" term.

The sequence rule for these shirts is "add two to each term to get the next term."

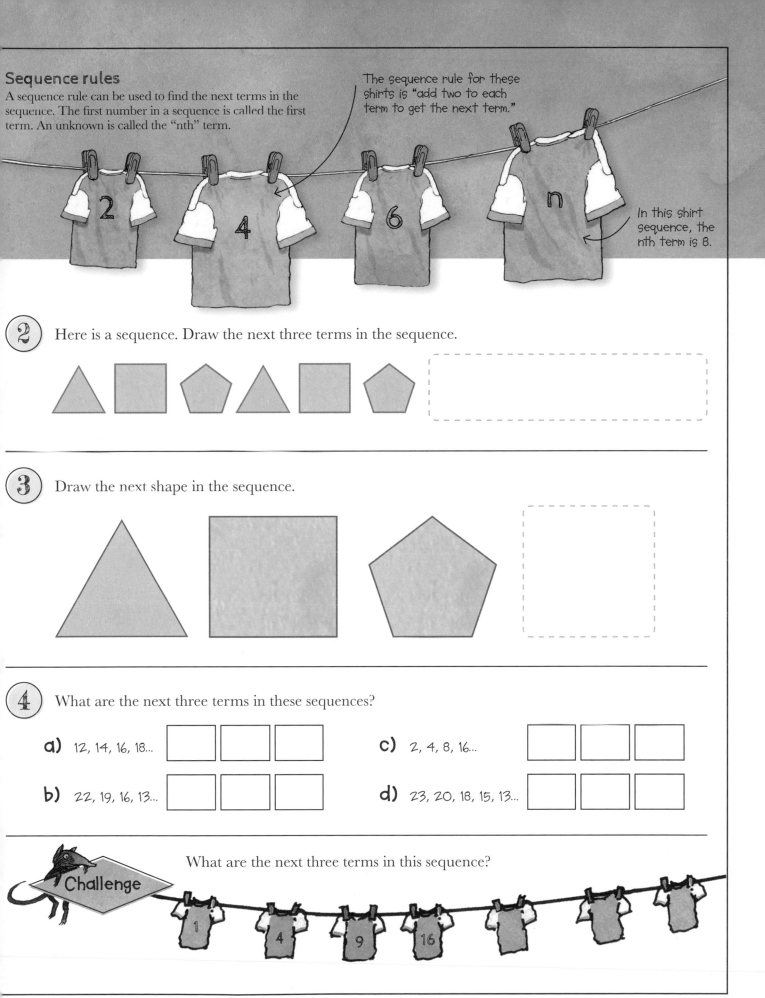

In this shirt sequence, the nth term is 8.

**2** Here is a sequence. Draw the next three terms in the sequence.

**3** Draw the next shape in the sequence.

**4** What are the next three terms in these sequences?

**a)** 12, 14, 16, 18...

**c)** 2, 4, 8, 16...

**b)** 22, 19, 16, 13...

**d)** 23, 20, 18, 15, 13...

**Challenge** What are the next three terms in this sequence?

1    4    9    16

71

# Angles

We describe how far something has turned in a particular direction using angles. Angles measure the distance between two lines that meet at a point. We measure angles using a unit called degrees. The symbol for a degree is "°."

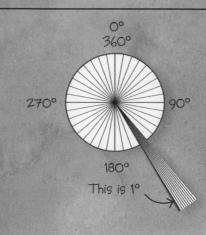

**Measuring with degrees**
A full turn is divided up into 360 equal-sized degrees. That means that 1 degree is equal to 1/360 of a full turn. A quarter turn (right angle) is 90° and a half turn is 180°.

The elephant shrews have set up a device to water their carrots. The mammoth is using this to show the shrews the different types of angles. Write the name of each type of angle shown.

**a)** _____ angle   **b)** _____ angle   **c)** _____ angle   **d)** _____ angle

Angles are formed when two or more lines meet or cross over.

1. Draw lines to match the elephant shrews' drawings to the number of angles they have. The first one has been done for you.

**a)**    **b)**   **c)**   **d)**   **e)**

O     1     2     3     4

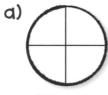

2. For each of the circles below, color in the angle given.

**a)**   **b)**   **c)**   **d)**   **e)**

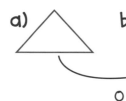            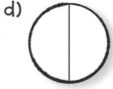

Right angle     Acute angle     Obtuse angle     Straight angle     Reflex angle

72

## Types of angles

Angles are named according to their size. Some of the most important angles are shown here.

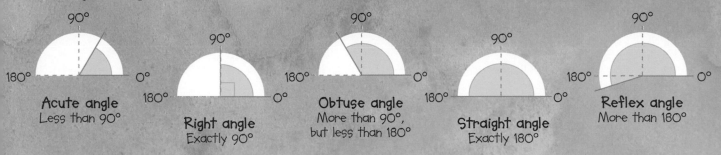

**Acute angle**
Less than 90°

**Right angle**
Exactly 90°

**Obtuse angle**
More than 90°, but less than 180°

**Straight angle**
Exactly 180°

**Reflex angle**
More than 180°

**3** Color in the smallest angle in each diagram.

a)

b)

c)

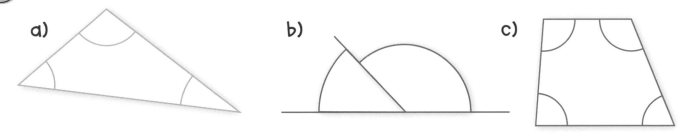

**4** Use the symbols >, <, or = to compare these pairs of angles. The first one has been done for you.

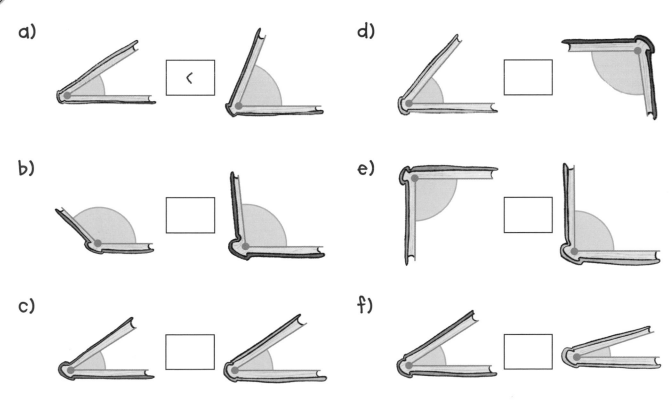

a) $<$

b)

c)

d)

e)

f)

73

## 5

Look at these protractors and identify the angles that are shaded, then answer the questions. The first one has been done for you.

a)

What is this angle? `135°`

What type of angle is it? ___Obtuse___

Use a protractor to measure angles in degrees.

50°

b)

What is this angle?

What type of angle is it? _____

c)

What is this angle?

What type of angle is it? _____

d)

What is this angle?

What type of angle is it? _____

## 6

Draw lines to match the angles with the correct description.

37°

180°

154°

279°

90°

Obtuse angle

Right angle

Reflex angle

Acute angle

Straight angle

74

**7** Use a protractor to measure the size of these angles.

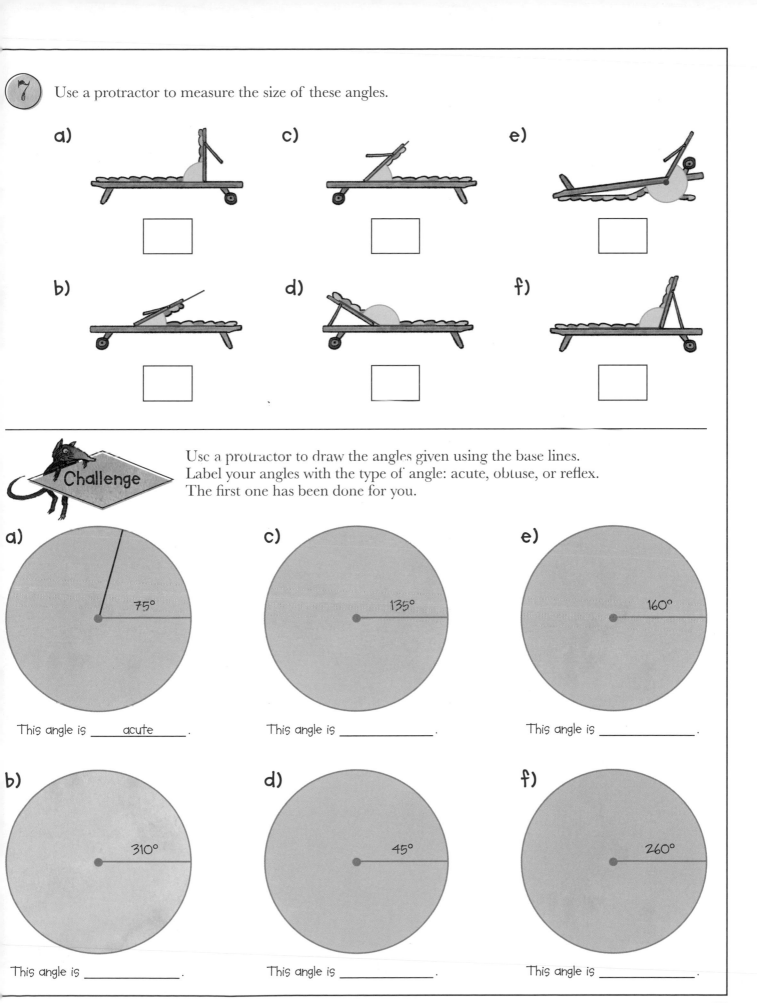

a)

c)

e)

b)

d)

f)

**Challenge**

Use a protractor to draw the angles given using the base lines.
Label your angles with the type of angle: acute, obtuse, or reflex.
The first one has been done for you.

a)

75°

This angle is ____acute____ .

c)

135°

This angle is _____ .

e)

160°

This angle is _____ .

b)

310°

This angle is _____ .

d)

45°

This angle is _____ .

f)

260°

This angle is _____ .

# Symmetry

A shape or an object is symmetrical when it is the same on both sides. The two halves are exact, mirror images of each other.

The butterfly has one line of symmetry.

Warm-up This mammoth is explaining reflective symmetry to the elephant shrews and has used a mirror to demonstrate the line of symmetry. Can you help the shrews by drawing the lines of symmetry on the other objects they have found?

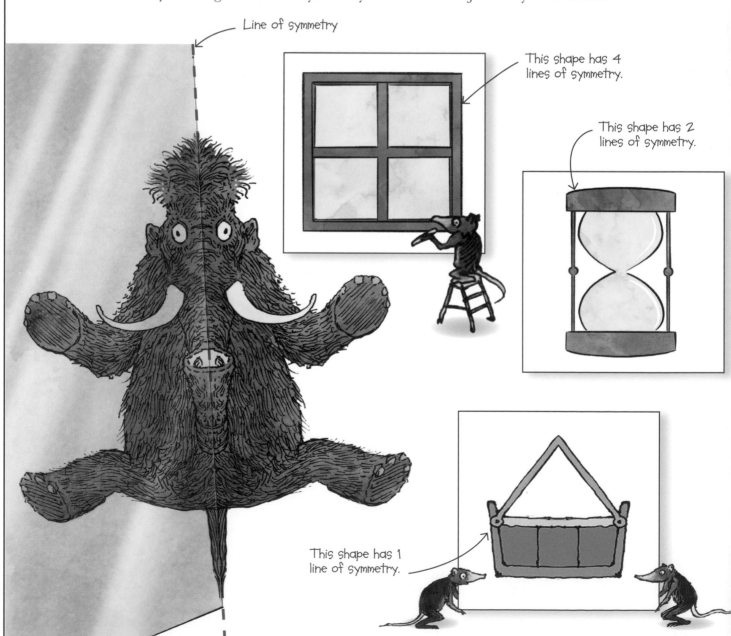

Line of symmetry

This shape has 4 lines of symmetry.

This shape has 2 lines of symmetry.

This shape has 1 line of symmetry.

## Reflective symmetry

If you can divide a shape into two identical halves that fit perfectly onto each other, then the shape has reflective symmetry. A shape can have several lines of reflective symmetry.

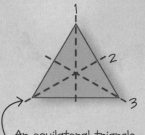

An equilateral triangle has 3 lines of reflective symmetry.

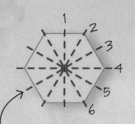

A hexagon has 6 lines of reflective symmetry.

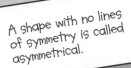

A shape with no lines of symmetry is called asymmetrical.

### Practice

**1** Use a mirror to draw lines of symmetry on these shapes.

a)
b)
c)
d)
e)
f)

**2** How many lines of symmetry do these shapes have?

a)  
b)  
c)  
d)

**3** Circle the triangle below that does not have a line of symmetry.

a)
b)
c)

**4** Use a mirror to draw lines of symmetry on these shapes.

a)
b)
c)

### Challenge

The number 3 has one line of symmetry. Which number between 1 and 9 has the most lines of symmetry?

Draw the number and the lines of symmetry in the box.

# Transformations

Shapes can be moved in lots of different ways. Changing the position of a shape or the way it points is called a transformation. The three most common transformations are translation, reflection, and rotation.

**Translation**
Translation is when an object is moved to a new position without changing its shape or size.

## Warm-up

The elephant shrews are showing the mammoths the difference between translation, reflection, and rotation. Help them by filling in the blanks to give the type of transformation for each shrew.

**a)**

This is a

_____.

**b)**

This is a

_____.

**c)**

This is a

_____.

A turn can go in two different directions. Imagine you are turning the hands on a clock. "Clockwise" is the way the hands normally move. "Counterclockwise" is the opposite direction.

Counterclockwise

Clockwise

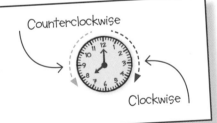

## Practice

1) Shade the circle after each of the turns shown. The first one has been done for you.

**a)**

A quarter turn clockwise

**b)**

A quarter turn clockwise

**c)**

A half turn clockwise

**d)**

A half turn clockwise

## Reflection

A reflection is a type of transformation where an object is moved to make a new, mirror image of the original object.

## Rotation

This type of transformation is called rotation. The mammoth shape has been turned around a point (the center of rotation). The amount the shape is rotated is called the angle of rotation.

Center of rotation

**2** What transformation is shown by each of these pictures?

a)

b)

c)

**3** This windmill has been turned in three different ways. Color in how the sails will look after each turn.

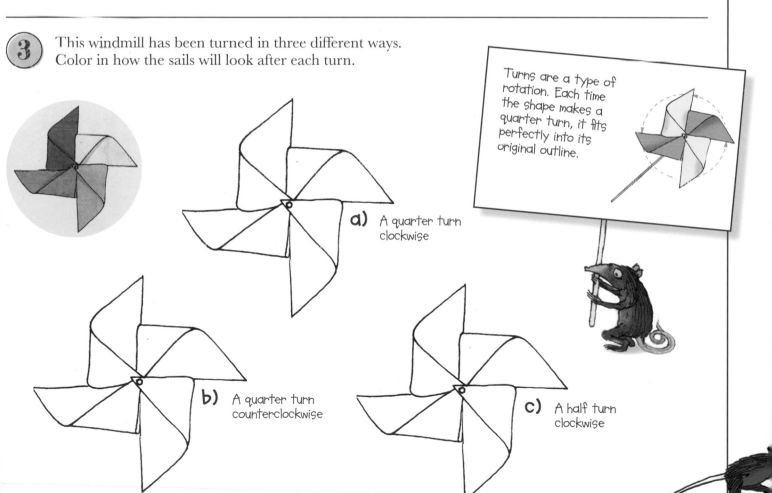

Turns are a type of rotation. Each time the shape makes a quarter turn, it fits perfectly into its original outline.

a) A quarter turn clockwise

b) A quarter turn counterclockwise

c) A half turn clockwise

**4** Translate the shapes according to the instructions. Draw the new position of the shapes on the grids.

**a)** 5 squares to the right and 4 squares up.

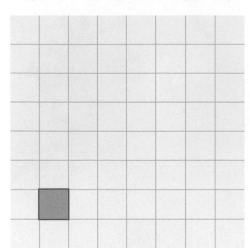

**b)** 4 squares down and 3 squares to the left.

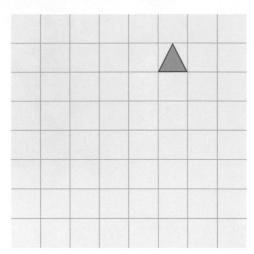

**5** Reflect the shapes in the dotted line. Draw the reflected shapes on the grids.

**a)**

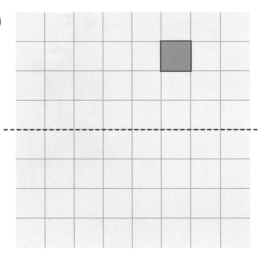

**b)**

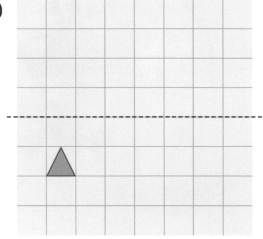

**6** The mammoths have made a flag. Rotate it through a quarter turn counterclockwise about the center of rotation shown by the x.

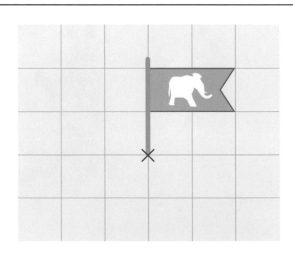

**7** The elephant shrews have made a triangular flag. Rotate it through a quarter turn clockwise about the center of rotation shown by the x.

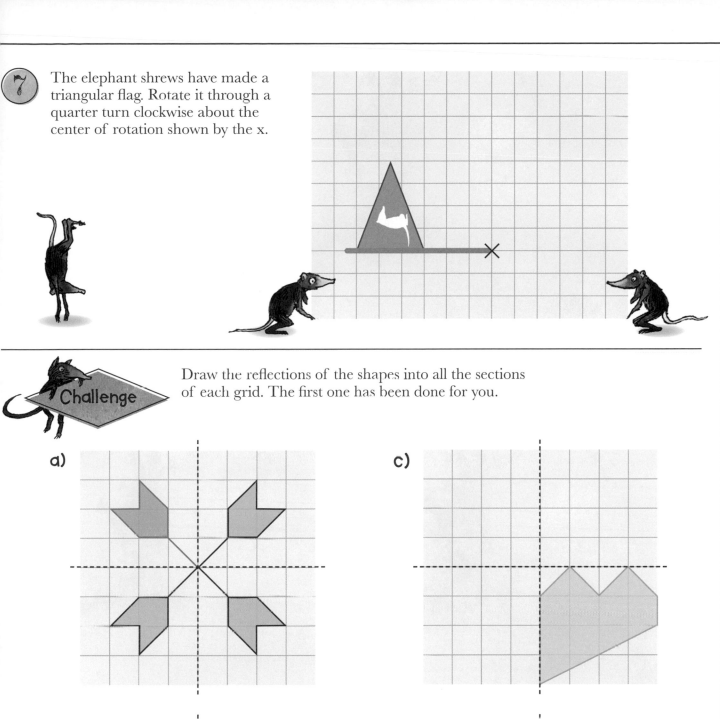

**Challenge**

Draw the reflections of the shapes into all the sections of each grid. The first one has been done for you.

a)

c)

b)

d)

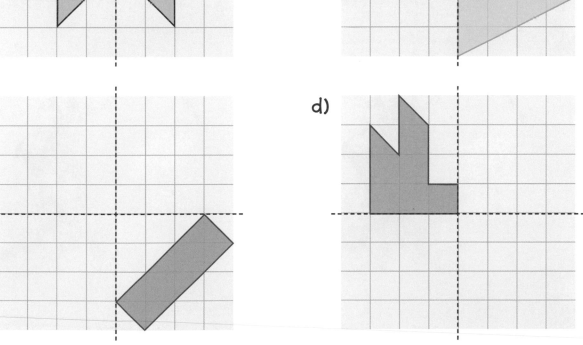

# Lines

A line is something that joins two points. Lines can be straight or curved. A straight line can point in any direction. You can measure the length of a line, but it doesn't have height or thickness.

There are lots of lines in the structure of this roller coaster. Fill in the blanks to help the elephant shrews understand the types of lines they can see.

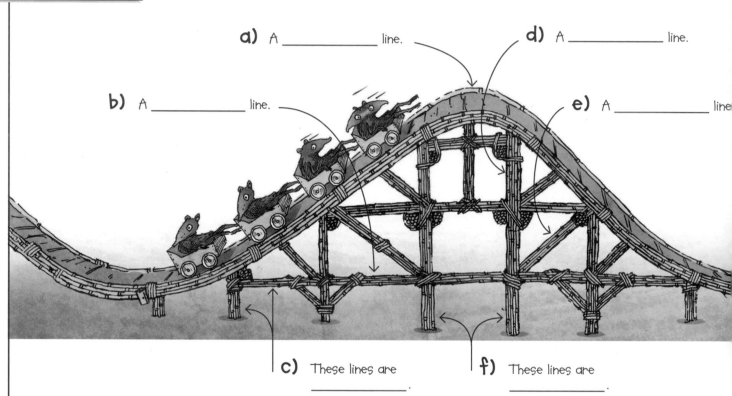

a) A _____ line.

b) A _____ line.

d) A _____ line.

e) A _____ line

c) These lines are _____.

f) These lines are _____.

## Practice

1  Draw an example of each different type of line.

a) Horizontal

b) Vertical

c) Diagonal

d) Curved

## Types of lines

We use different words to describe different types of lines.

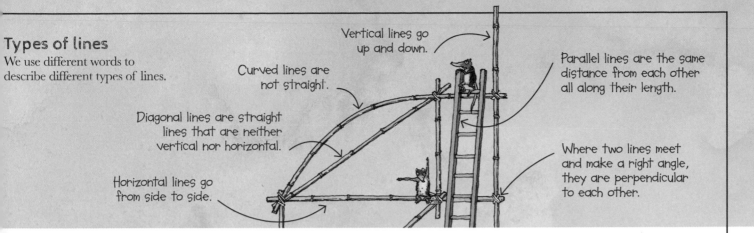

Vertical lines go up and down.

Curved lines are not straight.

Diagonal lines are straight lines that are neither vertical nor horizontal.

Horizontal lines go from side to side.

Parallel lines are the same distance from each other all along their length.

Where two lines meet and make a right angle, they are perpendicular to each other.

**2** For each of these shapes, count the number of horizontal (H), vertical (V), and diagonal (D) lines. The first one has been done for you.

| H | 2 | | | |
|---|---|---|---|---|
| V | 2 | | | |
| D | 2 | | | |

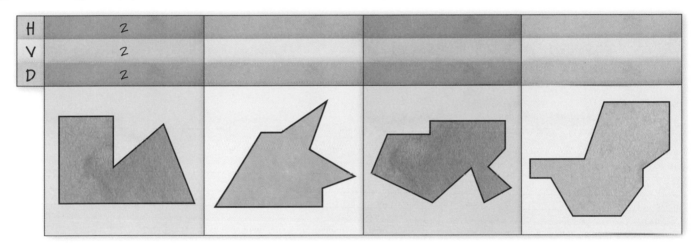

**3** Draw a circle around the parallel lines.

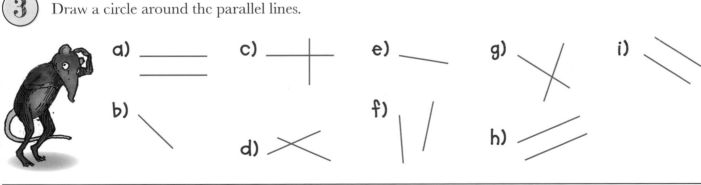

a)   c)   e)   g)   i)

b)   d)   f)   h)

**4** Draw a circle around the perpendicular lines.

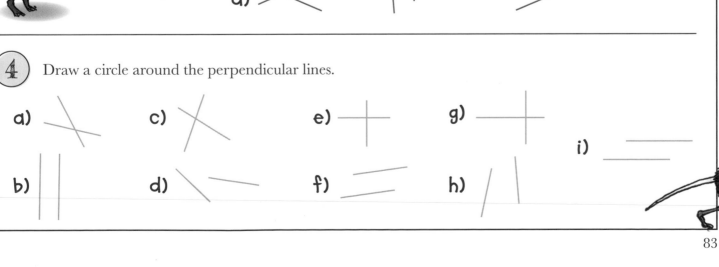

a)   c)   e)   g)

b)   d)   f)   h)   i)

83

**5** Draw a line that is parallel to the lines below. The first one has been done for you.

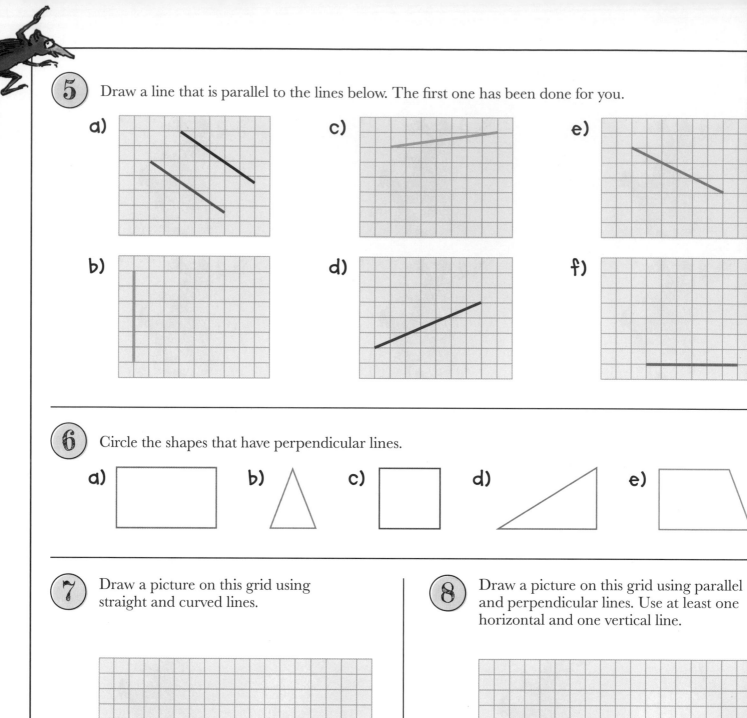

a)

c)

e)

b)

d)

f)

---

**6** Circle the shapes that have perpendicular lines.

a) [rectangle]   b) [triangle]   c) [square]   d) [right triangle]   e) [trapezoid]

---

**7** Draw a picture on this grid using straight and curved lines.

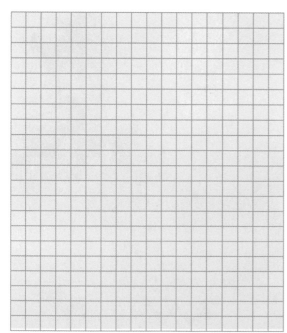

**8** Draw a picture on this grid using parallel and perpendicular lines. Use at least one horizontal and one vertical line.

**9** Measure these lines using string. Put them in order of length, with the shortest first.

a)

d)

b)

e)

f)

c)

[ ] [ ] [ ] [ ] [ ] [ ]

**10** Measure these lines using string and check off the longest in each pair.

a) [ ] ———————————  [ ] ～～～～

b) [ ] ⌒  [ ] ——

c) [ ] ◎  [ ] ————

**Challenge**

Draw a picture that uses at least four pairs of perpendicular lines and three horizontal lines.

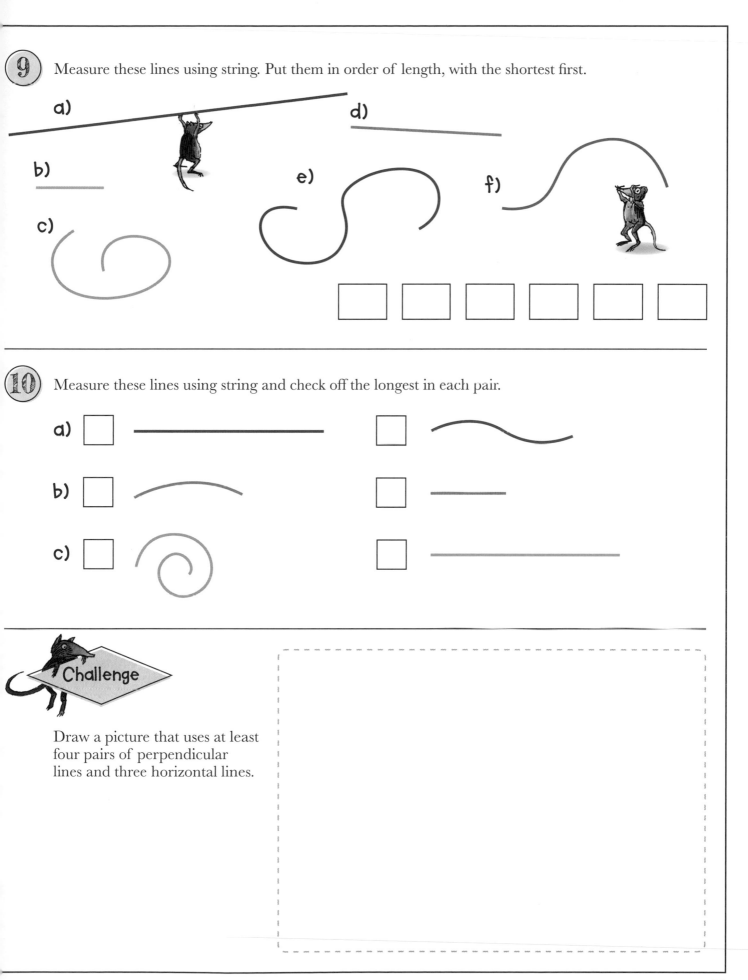

# 2D shapes

Shapes that are flat are called two-dimensional (or 2D) shapes. They have length and width but no thickness. 2D shapes can have straight sides, curved sides, or both.

**Polygon or not?**
2D shapes with only straight edges belong to a group called polygons. A 2D shape with one or more curved edges is not a polygon.

Polygon · Not a polygon · Polygon

**Warm-up** The mammoths are trying to work out which of these shapes are polygons. Can you help them by checking off the shapes that are polygons? The first one has been done for you.

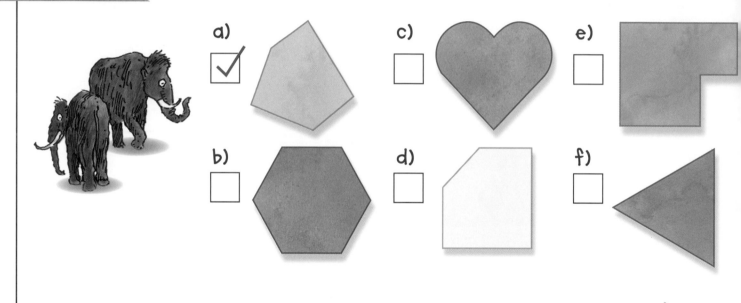

a) ✓

b)

c)

d)

e)

f)

**Practice**

1. Complete each connect-the-dot shape and unscramble the names of these regular polygons. The first one has been done for you.

a) **3** angles and sides — aglirTne — Triangle

b) **6** angles and sides — exagonH — _____

c) **7** angles and sides — tagepHon — _____

d) **4** angles and sides — alQraudteira — _____

e) **8** angles and sides — atgocnO — _____

f) **5** angles and sides — nePotagn — _____

g) **9** angles and sides — onNagon — _____

## Regular and irregular

There are two types of polygons.
Regular polygons have sides of
equal length and equal angles.
Irregular polygons have sides of
different lengths and angles that
are not always equal.

Regular
octagon

Irregular
octagon

In every polygon, regular
or irregular, the number
of sides is the same as
the number of angles.

**2** Draw lines to match the shapes to the correct name.

a)

b)

c)

d)

e)

Decagon

Quadrilateral

Triangle

Nonagon

Heptagon

**Challenge**

Read the descriptions below
and write the letter of each
shape being described in
the box.

a)

b)

c)

d)

☐ A regular polygon
with 8 sides

☐ An irregular polygon
with 5 angles

☐ An irregular polygon
with 4 sides

☐ A regular polygon
with 4 corners

# Triangles

A triangle is a 2D shape with straight edges. It has three sides, three angles, and three vertices. It is also a polygon and has the smallest number of sides of all polygons.

Warm-up

The mammoth is stomping across the triangle bridge, looking for the four different types of triangles. Can you spot them all?

Draw circles in different colors around the four types of triangles. Use blue for equilateral, green for isosceles, yellow for right, and red for scalene.

## Practice

**1** Check off the box next to the equilateral triangle.

a)
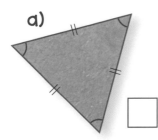
☐

b)
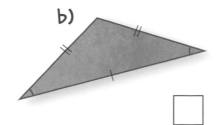
☐

c)
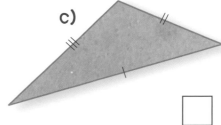
☐

# Types of triangles

There are four main types of triangles: equilateral (all the sides and angles are equal), right (one angle is a right angle), isosceles (two equal sides and two equal angles), and scalene (all sides and angles are different).

**Equal sides**
Two dashes show sides with equal length.

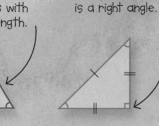

Equilateral triangle

**Right angles**
This sign means it is a right angle.

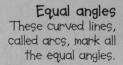

Right triangle

**Equal angles**
These curved lines, called arcs, mark all the equal angles.

Isosceles triangle

**Unequal sides**
Different dashes show that each side in this triangle is different.

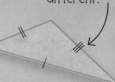

Scalene triangle

---

**② Check off the box next to the isosceles triangle.**

a) 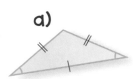 ☐

b)  ☐

c)  ☐

---

**③**

a) Draw a red circle around the scalene triangle.

b) Draw a black circle around the right triangle.

  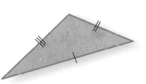 

---

**④ Draw lines to match the name of each triangle with the correct shape.**

| Equilateral triangle | Scalene triangle | Isosceles triangle | Right triangle |

a)

b)

c)

d)

---

**Challenge**

Use six straws of three different lengths similar to those shown. Investigate the types of triangles you can make with your straws. Draw the triangles in the box.

# Angles in triangles

There are three angles in a triangle. In any triangle, all the angles add up to 180°. You can test this by rearranging the angles of a triangle to make a straight line, which also measures 180°.

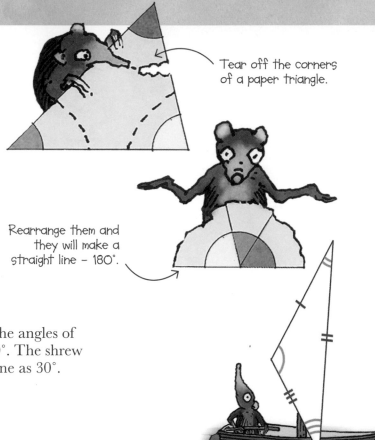

Tear off the corners of a paper triangle.

## Warm-up

The mammoths have told the elephant shrews that angles in a triangle always add up to 180°. They check this by arranging the angles of a triangle into a straight line. Follow these instructions and see for yourself. It doesn't matter what kind of triangle you use, this will always work.

Rearrange them and they will make a straight line – 180°.

## Practice

 The elephant shrew wants to check that the angles of the triangular sail really do add up to 180°. The shrew measures one of the angles as 125° and one as 30°. What will the third angle measure?

$$180° - 125° - 30° = \boxed{\phantom{00}}$$

2) Find the missing angles in these triangles.

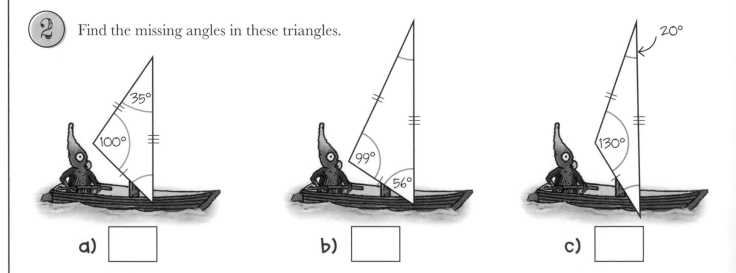

a) $\boxed{\phantom{00}}$

b) $\boxed{\phantom{00}}$

c) $\boxed{\phantom{00}}$

90

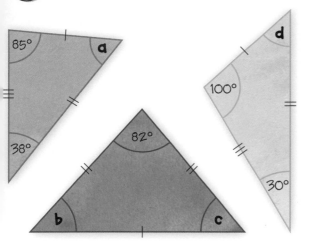
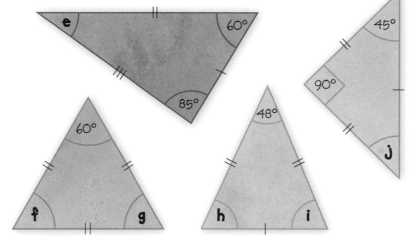

**3** Find the missing angles in these triangles.

85°  a

38°

100°

82°

b       c

30°

d

e       60°

85°

60°

f       g

48°

h       i

45°

90°

j

| a) ☐ | c) ☐ | e) ☐ | g) ☐ | i) ☐ |
| b) ☐ | d) ☐ | f) ☐ | h) ☐ | j) ☐ |

---

**4** Fill in the missing angles in the calculations below.

a)  180° = 27° + 90° + ☐

c)  180° = 99° + 54° + ☐

e)  180° = 44° + 55° + ☐

b)  180° = 34° + 75° + ☐

d)  180° = 25° + 85° + ☐

f)  180° = 129° + 24° + ☐

---

**5** Check off the boxes for the angle sums that do not describe a triangle.

a)  50° + 30° + 100°  ☐

d)  40° + 30° + 110°  ☐

g)  50° + 30° + 90°  ☐

b)  50° + 40° + 100°  ☐

e)  50° + 20° + 100°  ☐

h)  20° + 40° + 120°  ☐

c)  60° + 30° + 90°  ☐

f)  40° + 40° + 100°  ☐

i)  100° + 10° + 20°  ☐

---

**Challenge**

Look at this isosceles triangle that is sitting inside a rectangle.

Work out angles a and b.

a = ☐     b = ☐

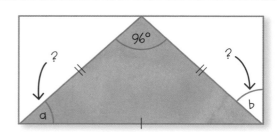

96°

?        ?

a        b

91

# Quadrilaterals

A quadrilateral is a 2D polygon with four sides, four angles, and four vertices (points where lines meet—like a corner). Quadrilaterals can have equal sides and angles or have sides and angles that are different from each other. Some quadrilaterals are parallelograms and some are not.

The mammoths are showing the elephant shrews what different quadrilateral shapes are called. Draw lines to match the names and shapes of these quadrilaterals.

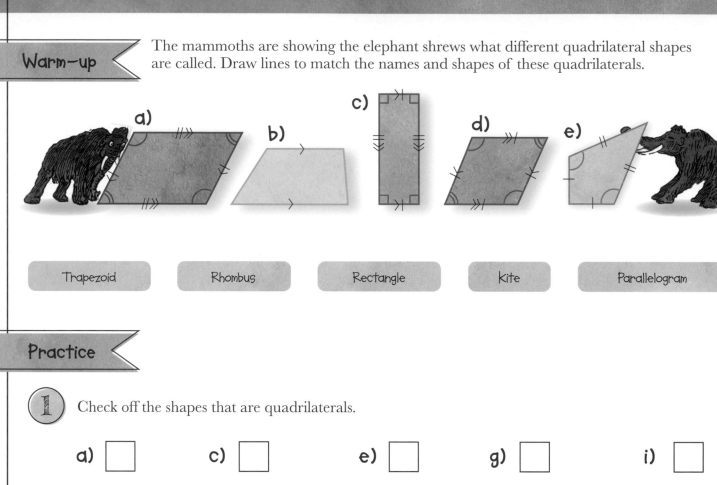

a)    b)    c)    d)    e)

Trapezoid    Rhombus    Rectangle    Kite    Parallelogram

1. Check off the shapes that are quadrilaterals.

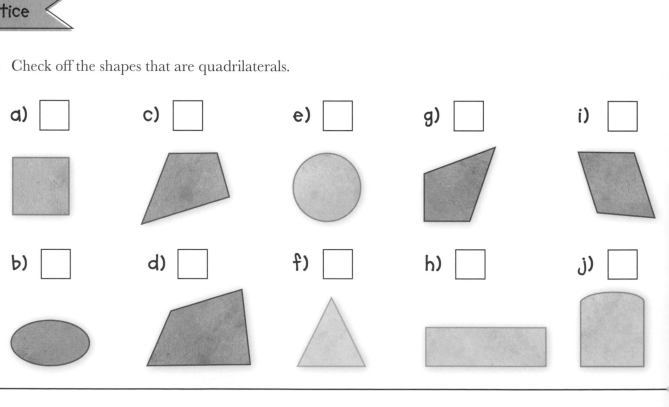

a) ☐    c) ☐    e) ☐    g) ☐    i) ☐

b) ☐    d) ☐    f) ☐    h) ☐    j) ☐

# Name that shape!

Squares and rectangles are two common quadrilaterals. Other examples are parallelograms, rhombuses, kites, trapezoids, and irregular quadrilaterals.

**Parallelogram**

Parallelograms have two sets of parallel sides. We show parallel sides with arrows.

Equal angles are marked with arcs.

A trapezoid has one pair of parallel sides.

**Trapezoid**

**Irregular quadrilateral**

A rhombus has four sides that are equal in length. We show this with dashes.

**Rhombus**

**Kite**

A kite shape has two long sides of equal length and two short sides of equal length.

This quadrilateral has no parallel sides, no equal angles, and no edges of equal length.

---

**2)** Draw a rhombus with sides equal to 3 squares on the grid.

**3)** Circle the quadrilaterals that have four right angles.

a)  c)  e)

b)  d)  f)

---

**4)** Divide each of the quadrilaterals into two triangles. The first one has been done for you.

a)  b)  c)  d)  e)  f)

---

**5)** All quadrilaterals can be split into two triangles. Fill in the blanks below.

**a)** Each triangle has an angle sum of ☐ .

**b)** This means that the angle sum of a quadrilateral is 2 × ☐ = ☐

The triangle test shows that the angles in a quadrilateral always add up to 360°. All quadrilaterals can be divided into two triangles. A triangle's angles always add up to 180°, so 2 × 180° = 360°.

---

**Challenge**

Find the missing angles in these quadrilaterals.

**a)** 110°  70°  a  110°  ☐

**b)** 100°  80°  80°  b  ☐

**c)** 115°  90°  65°  c  ☐

93

# Circles

A circle is a 2D shape that does not have any vertices. It has one edge that is a curved line that goes all the way around a center point. This is called the circumference. Every point on the circumference is the same distance from the center. This distance is called the radius.

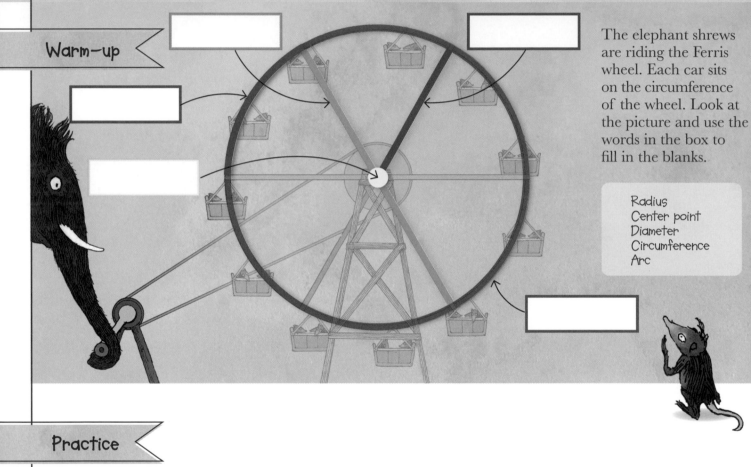

The elephant shrews are riding the Ferris wheel. Each car sits on the circumference of the wheel. Look at the picture and use the words in the box to fill in the blanks.

Radius
Center point
Diameter
Circumference
Arc

## Practice

1  Draw lines to match each word with its meaning.

a)  Circumference          Part of the circumference

b)  Radius          Distance all the way around the circle

c)  Diameter          Distance from center of circle to circumference

d)  Arc          Distance across circle through center

94

## Parts of a circle

Understanding the different parts of a circle help us measure its circumference. We can work out the circumference of a circle if we know its diameter: circumference = diameter × Pi (3.14). If we know the radius and not the diameter, we can still find the circumference because diameter = 2 × radius.

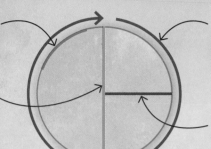

**Arc**
An arc is a section of the circumference.

**Circumference**
The distance all the way around a circle's perimeter (rim).

**Diameter**
A straight line that starts and finishes on the circumference and goes through the center point.

**Radius**
A straight line from the circle's center to its circumference.

---

 On each of these three circles, draw the part of the circle that is given below it.

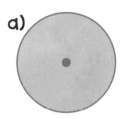 a)

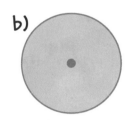 b)

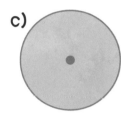 c)

Radius

Diameter

An arc

---

 On this circle, color the circumference in red. Draw one radius in blue. Draw another radius in green 45° from that radius. You can use a protractor to help you.

---

 Multiply these diameters by 3.14 (the value of Pi) to find the circumference of each circle. You can use a calculator to help you. The first one has been done for you.

If you measure the circumference of any circle, it will always be equal to the diameter multiplied by 3.14. This number is given a special name, Pi. Its symbol is "π."

 π

5 cm

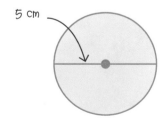

20 m

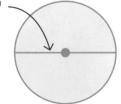

60 mm

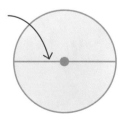

**a)** Circumference =

| 5 | × 3.14 = | 15.7 | cm |

**b)** Circumference =

| | × 3.14 = | | m |

**c)** Circumference =

| | × 3.14 = | | mm |

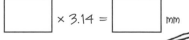
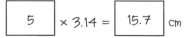
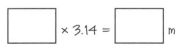

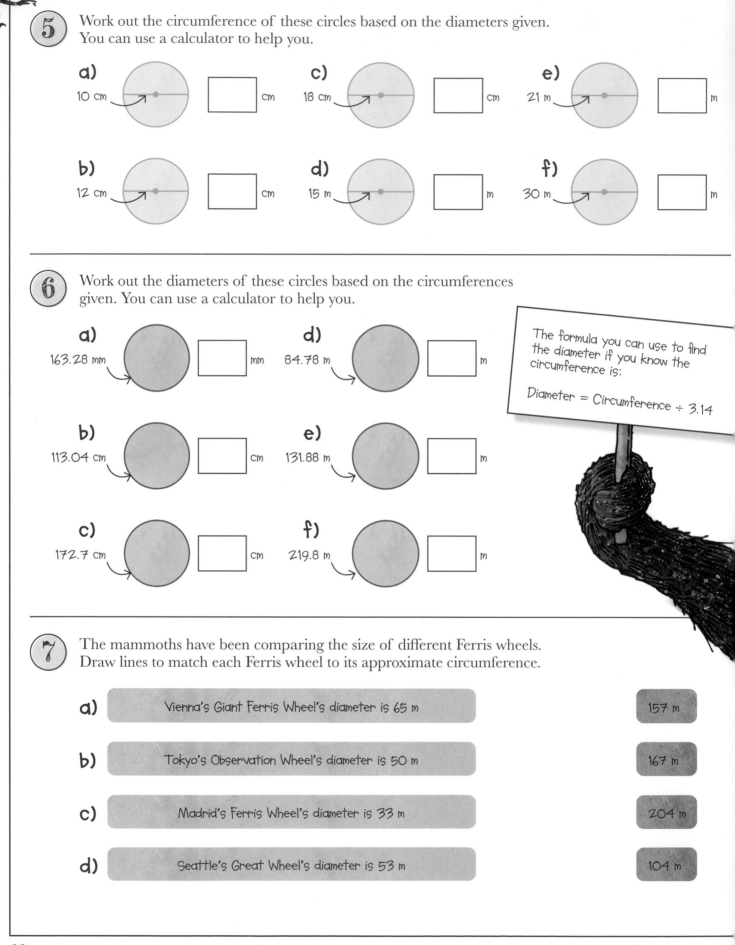

**5** Work out the circumference of these circles based on the diameters given.
You can use a calculator to help you.

a) 10 cm [    ] cm

b) 12 cm [    ] cm

c) 18 cm [    ] cm

d) 15 m [    ] m

e) 21 m [    ] m

f) 30 m [    ] m

**6** Work out the diameters of these circles based on the circumferences
given. You can use a calculator to help you.

a) 163.28 mm [    ] mm

b) 113.04 cm [    ] cm

c) 172.7 cm [    ] cm

d) 84.78 m [    ] m

e) 131.88 m [    ] m

f) 219.8 m [    ] m

The formula you can use to find the diameter if you know the circumference is:

Diameter = Circumference ÷ 3.14

**7** The mammoths have been comparing the size of different Ferris wheels.
Draw lines to match each Ferris wheel to its approximate circumference.

a) Vienna's Giant Ferris Wheel's diameter is 65 m

b) Tokyo's Observation Wheel's diameter is 50 m

c) Madrid's Ferris Wheel's diameter is 33 m

d) Seattle's Great Wheel's diameter is 53 m

157 m

167 m

204 m

104 m

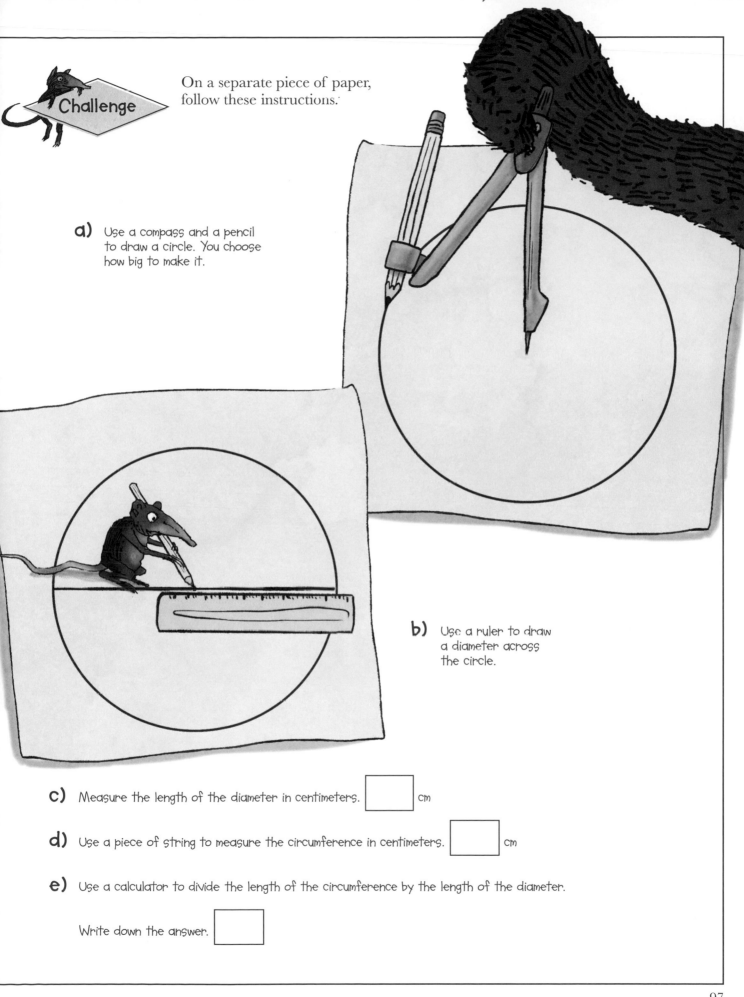

**Challenge**

On a separate piece of paper, follow these instructions.

**a)** Use a compass and a pencil to draw a circle. You choose how big to make it.

**b)** Use a ruler to draw a diameter across the circle.

**c)** Measure the length of the diameter in centimeters. [ ] cm

**d)** Use a piece of string to measure the circumference in centimeters. [ ] cm

**e)** Use a calculator to divide the length of the circumference by the length of the diameter.

Write down the answer. [ ]

# 3D shapes

Shapes that are solid are called three-dimensional (3D) shapes. They have length, width, and height. Unlike 2D shapes, which are flat, they take up space. A 3D shape also has edges, faces, and vertices.

**Face**
The surface of a 3D object is a face. It can be flat or curved.

**Edge**
An edge is the line where two or more faces of a 3D shape meet.

**Vertex**
A vertex is a corner. It's where two or more edges meet. Vertices is the plural of vertex.

Warm-up

The elephant shrews are building a model of a mammoth using 3D shapes. Can you help them identify these shapes by adding the correct labels from the box?

| Cuboid | Cylinder | Cube | Hemisphere |
| --- | --- | --- | --- |

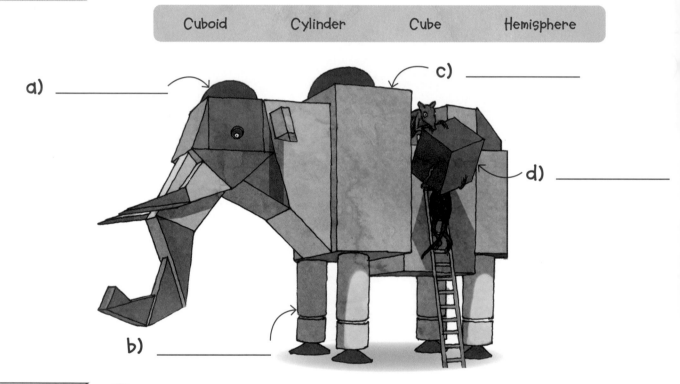

a) _____

c) _____

d) _____

b) _____

Practice

1  Use the words in the box to help you label the features of these shapes.

| Width | Length | Height | Edge | Vertex | Face |
| --- | --- | --- | --- | --- | --- |

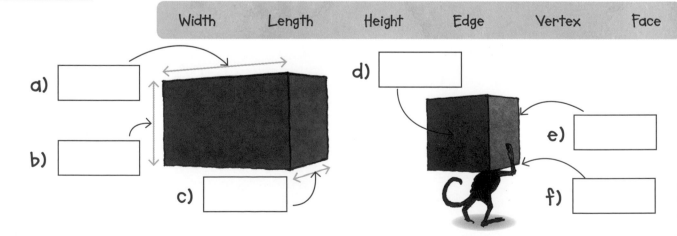

a) _____

b) _____

c) _____

d) _____

e) _____

f) _____

**2** Draw lines to match the names to each of these 3D shapes.

| Pyramid | Cuboid | Sphere | Hemisphere |
|---------|--------|--------|------------|

a)

b)

c)

d)

---

**3** How many faces do each of these shapes have?

a) ☐

c) ☐

b) ☐

d) ☐

**4** How many edges do each of these shapes have?

a) ☐

c) ☐

b) ☐

d) ☐

---

**Challenge**

Name the shapes from these descriptions.

a) A 3D shape with no edges or vertices and just one face. _____

b) A 3D shape that has four triangular faces. _____

c) A 3D shape that has six rectangular faces. _____

# Nets

When you open out a 3D shape and lay it out flat, you are left with a 2D shape called a net.

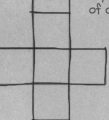
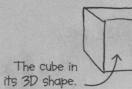
**Warm-up**

The elephant shrews have used the net of a cube to build a 3D cube. Can you answer their questions?

**a)** What shape are the faces of a cube? _____

**b)** How many faces are there? ☐

**Practice**

**1** The elephant shrews are trying to match up the shapes with the correct net. Draw lines to show them the right answers.

Triangular prism     Pyramid     Cylinder     Cuboid

**a)**     **b)**     **c)**     **d)**

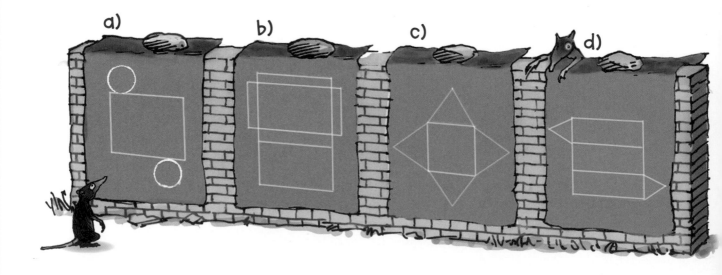

## Making a cube
A net can be cut out
and folded up to make
the 3D shape.

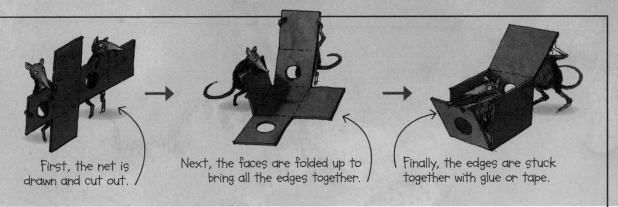

First, the net is
drawn and cut out.

Next, the faces are folded up to
bring all the edges together.

Finally, the edges are stuck
together with glue or tape.

 The elephant shrews know there is more than one net that makes
a square pyramid shape. Circle all the square pyramid nets.

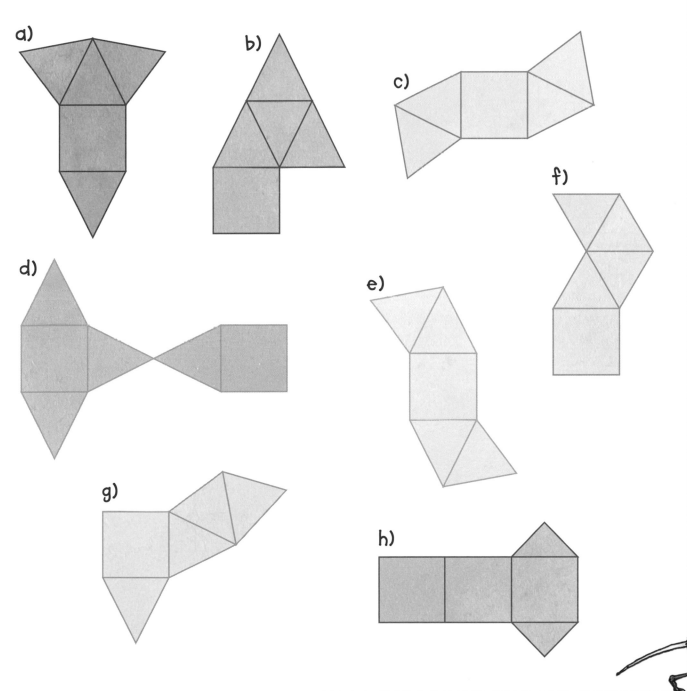

a)

b)

c)

f)

d)

e)

g)

h)

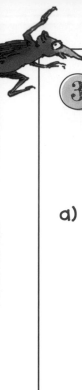

**3** Circle the correct net shape for each of these objects.

a)

i)
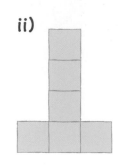

ii)
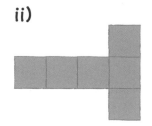

iii)
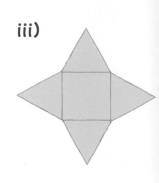

b)

i)
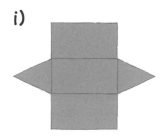

ii)
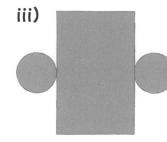

iii)

c)

i)
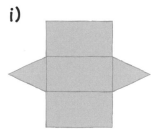

ii)
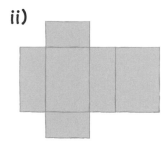

iii)
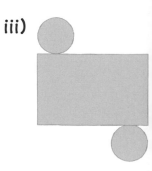

d)
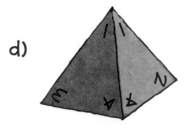

i)
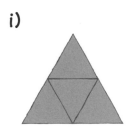

ii)
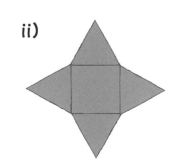

iii)
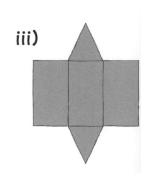

**4** There are 11 different nets that make a cube. Some of them are given below, but not all the nets will give a cube. Circle all the nets that form a cube.

You could copy the nets and try making the shapes if that helps.

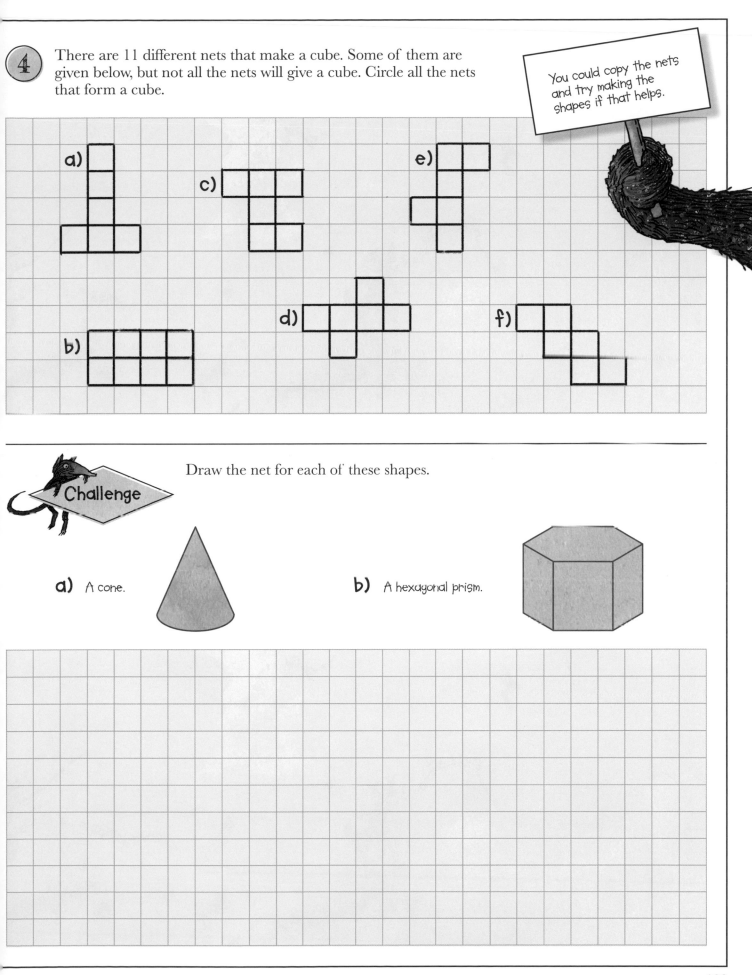

a)

c)

e)

b)

d)

f)

**Challenge**

Draw the net for each of these shapes.

a) A cone.

b) A hexagonal prism.

# Length

Length is the distance between two points. Units of length include millimeters (mm), centimeters (cm), meters (m), and kilometers (km). When measuring 3D objects, we also use words like "width" and "height" to describe distances.

Warm-up

The mammoth is getting ready to carve a statue. The elephant shrews have measured the size of the block. It is 4 m high, 7 m long, and 3.5 m wide. Can you fill in the blanks to show the mammoth which measurement is which?

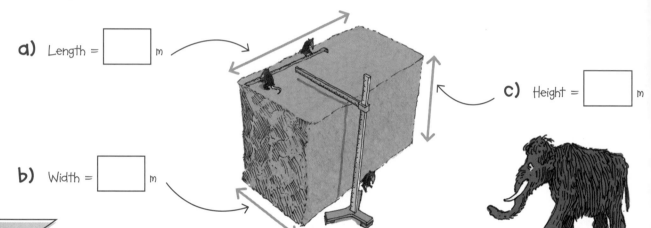

a) Length = ☐ m

b) Width = ☐ m

c) Height = ☐ m

Practice

1) Measure the length or height of these objects using a ruler.

a) Length = ☐ cm

b) Height = ☐ cm

c) Length = ☐ cm

d) Height = ☐ cm

e) Height = ☐ cm

2) Order these lengths by size, starting with the smallest.

☐ ☐ ☐ ☐ ☐

4 mm    42 m

480 cm    480 mm    420 cm

## Converting units

It doesn't make sense to use the same units of measurement for very long and very short things, so we use millimeters for small things and kilometers for big things. The measurements are all related, and you can easily convert between them.

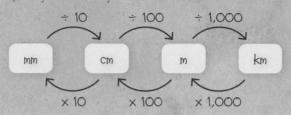

## Using a ruler

You can use a ruler to measure lengths. You must make sure that the ruler is lined up with the start of what you are measuring.

This line of cubes is 6 cm long.

---

**3** The elephant shrews are trying to convert between different units. Fill in the blanks for each conversion to show them the multiplication or division needed. The first one has been done for you.

**a)** m to cm    `× 100`

**b)** mm to cm    ☐

**c)** m to km    ☐

**d)** cm to mm    ☐

**e)** km to m    ☐

**f)** cm to m    ☐

---

**4** Some of these measurements are the same lengths but are written using different units. Draw lines to link the same distances. The first has been done for you.

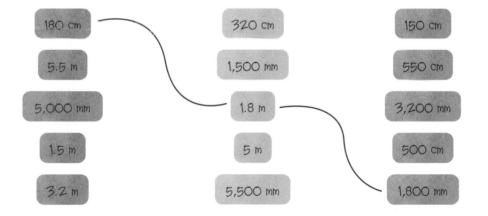

180 cm  320 cm  150 cm

5.5 m  1,500 mm  550 cm

5,000 mm  1.8 m  3,200 mm

1.5 m  5 m  500 cm

3.2 m  5,500 mm  1,800 mm

---

**Challenge**

Convert these lengths into meters.

**a)** 1.4 km = ☐ m

**b)** 480 mm = ☐ m

**c)** 3,700 cm = ☐ m

**d)** 15 cm = ☐ m

**e)** 6.8 km = ☐ m

**f)** 3.9 km = ☐ m

105

# Perimeter

The perimeter is the total distance around the sides of a 2D shape.
There are different ways to find the perimeter. You could measure
the length of all the sides or use formulas to calculate the perimeter.

Warm-up

The elephant shrews are trying to find the perimeter of these shapes.
Help them add up the lengths. The shapes are not drawn to scale.
The first one has been done for you.

**a)** Scalene triangle

Perimeter = | 3 | + | 5 | + | 6 | = | 14 | m

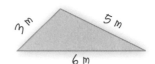

**b)** Square

Perimeter = [ ] + [ ] + [ ] + [ ] = [ ] cm

**c)** Parallelogram

Perimeter = [ ] + [ ] + [ ] + [ ] = [ ] cm

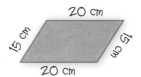

**d)** Equilateral triangle

Perimeter = [ ] + [ ] + [ ] = [ ] mm

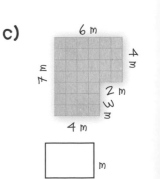

Practice

**1** For each of these shapes, use the lengths to work out the perimeter.
The shapes are not drawn to scale.

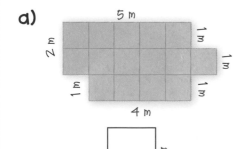

**a)**

[ ] m

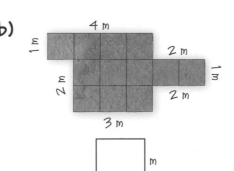

**b)**

[ ] m

**c)**

[ ] m

## Measuring the length

One way of working out the perimeter of a shape is to measure the length of each side, then add the lengths together.

The perimeter of this square is
9 m + 9 m + 9 m + 9 m = 36 m

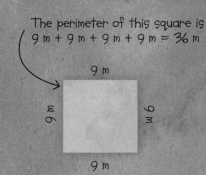

9 m

9 m

9 m

9 m

## Using formulas

You can also use formulas to help you calculate perimeters. Letters represent the sides of a shape.

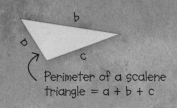

b

b

c

Perimeter of a scalene triangle = a + b + c

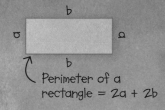

b

a

a

b

Perimeter of a rectangle = 2a + 2b

---

**2** Draw lines to match each perimeter formula with the correct shape.

| 5b | 2a + b | 2a + 2b | 4a |

**a)**
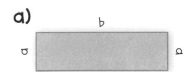
b
a
a
b

**b)**
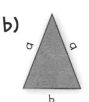
a
a
b

**c)**
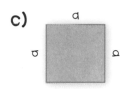
a
a
a
a

**d)**
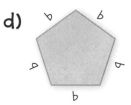
b
b
b
b
b

---

**3** Circle the shape described in each formula below.

**a)** Perimeter = a + b + c + d

**c)** Perimeter = 3a

**b)** Perimeter = 2a + 2b

---

Challenge

The mammoth says that all of these shapes have the same perimeter. The elephant shrew says they have different perimeters. The shapes are not drawn to scale. The sides of each shape are the same length.

Who is correct? Check the box.

Mammoth ☐   Elephant shrew ☐

Explain why. _____

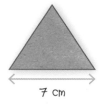  

3 cm         7 cm         4 cm

107

# Area

Area is the amount of space taken up by a 2D shape or surface. We measure area in square units. The square units we use most often are square millimeters (mm), square centimeters (cm), square meters (m), and square kilometers (km). There are two ways of finding the area of a square or rectangle: counting squares or using a formula.

We show that units are squared using a small 2, like this:

km²

## Warm-up

Each elephant shrew has a square patch in their garden where they grow their favorite fruits, flowers, and vegetables. They want to know how big the garden is in total. Can you help them by counting up the squares to find the size of the garden?

Each square is 1 m long and 1 m wide, or 1 m².

The whole garden is [ ] m².

## Practice

(1) Count the squares to find the areas of these shapes.

**a)** Area = [ ] squares

**b)** Area = [ ] squares

**c)** Area = [ ] squares

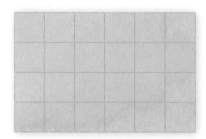

**d)** Area = [ ] squares

## Counting squares

You can divide up a square or rectangle into squares of the same size. If you know the size of each square, then you can find the area of the whole shape.

This rectangle is 10 squares in area. If each square is 1 m long and 1 m wide, then the rectangle is 10 m².

## Using a formula

To find the area of a square or rectangle, you multiply its length by its width. This is a formula, and we write it like this:
Area = Length x Width.

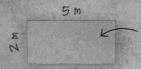

This rectangle is 5 m long by 2 m wide, so the area is 5 m x 2 m = 10 m².

---

 Count the squares to find the areas of these rectilinear shapes.

**a)** Area = ☐ squares

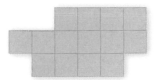

**b)** Area = ☐ squares

**c)** Area = ☐ squares

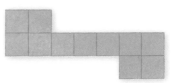

**d)** Area = ☐ squares

**e)** Area = ☐ squares

**f)** Area = ☐ squares

A rectilinear shape is a 2D, flat shape that has straight sides where all of the sides meet at right angles.

---

 Draw different shapes in each grid with the area shown. Each square represents 1 cm².

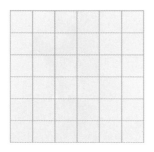

**a)** 4 cm²

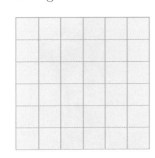

**b)** 18 cm²

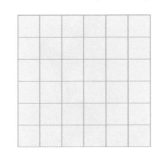

**c)** 6 cm²

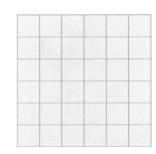

**d)** 12 cm²

**4**   The mammoths have drawn a map. Estimate how many squares the island covers.

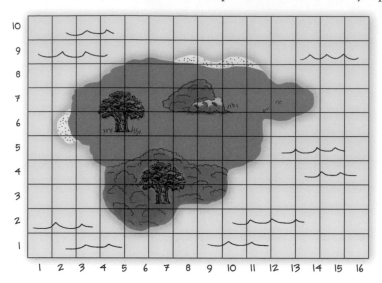

Count the whole squares first. Then count squares which are covered with a bit of island and divide that number by half. The estimated area = the whole squares + half the partially filled squares.

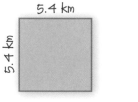

[    ] squares

---

**5**   Use the formula for the area of a square or rectangle to find the areas of these shapes.

 4 km, 2.5 km

 3 mm, 3 mm

 45 mm, 8 mm

**a)** _____ × _____ = _____ km²

**c)** _____ × _____ = _____ mm²

**e)** _____ × _____ = _____ mm²

 2.6 cm, 2.6 cm

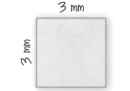 12 cm, 5.5 cm

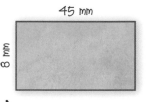 5.4 km, 5.4 km

**b)** _____ × _____ = _____ cm²

**d)** _____ × _____ = _____ cm²

**f)** _____ × _____ = _____ km²

---

**6**   Use the formula for the area of a square or rectangle to help you find the missing lengths of these shapes. The first one has been started for you.

Area = Length × Width
Length = Area ÷ Width
Width = Area ÷ Length

**a)**  [ a ] × [ 4 ] = [ 20 ]

[ 20 ] ÷ [ 4 ] = [ a ]

 4 cm, a, 20 cm²

a = [    ] cm

**b)**  [   ] × [   ] = [   ]

[   ] ÷ [   ] = [   ]

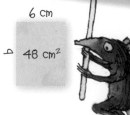 6 cm, b, 48 cm²

b = [    ] cm

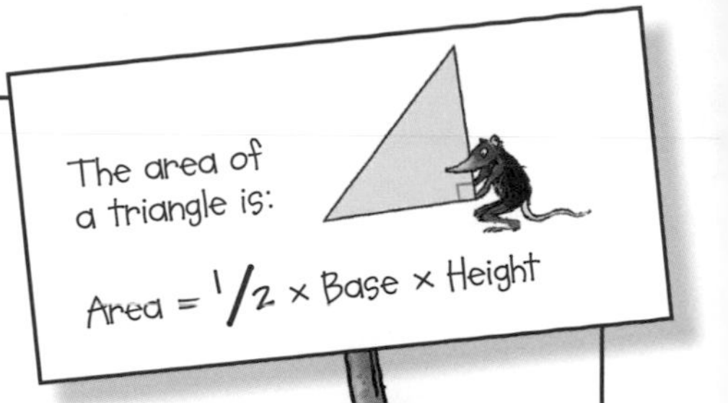

**7** Use the formula for the area of a triangle to help you find the area of these right triangles.

The area of a triangle is:

Area = ¹/₂ × Base × Height

**a)**
6 cm
5 cm

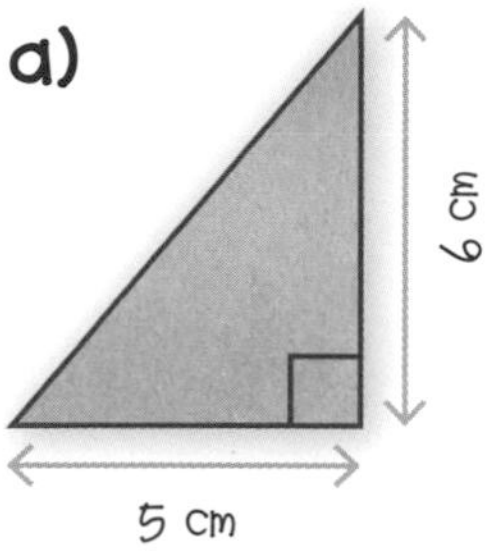

**b)**
2 cm
3 cm

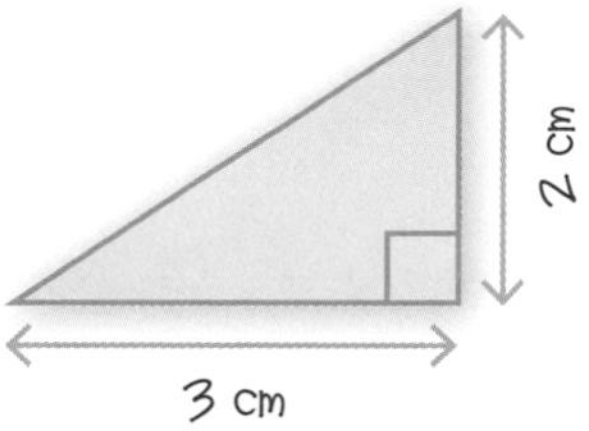

**c)**
4 cm
3 cm

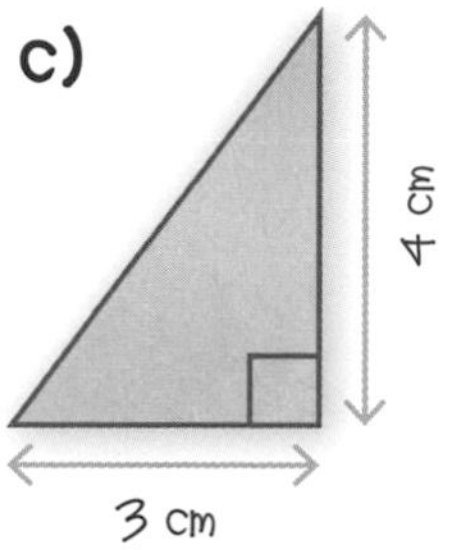

**d)**
5 cm
8 cm

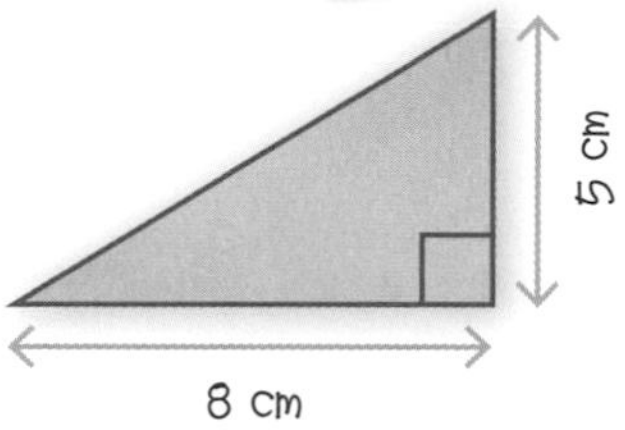

**8** Use the formula for the area of a triangle to help you find the area of these triangles.

**a)**
3 cm
6 cm

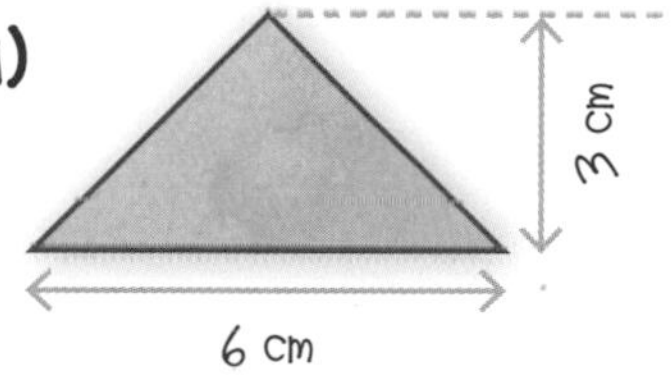

**c)**
2 cm
7 cm

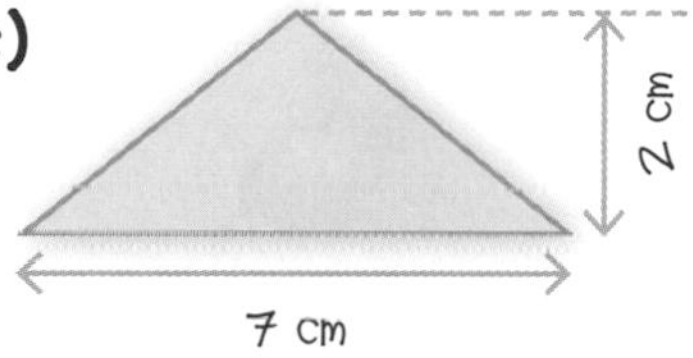

**e)**
9 cm
2 cm

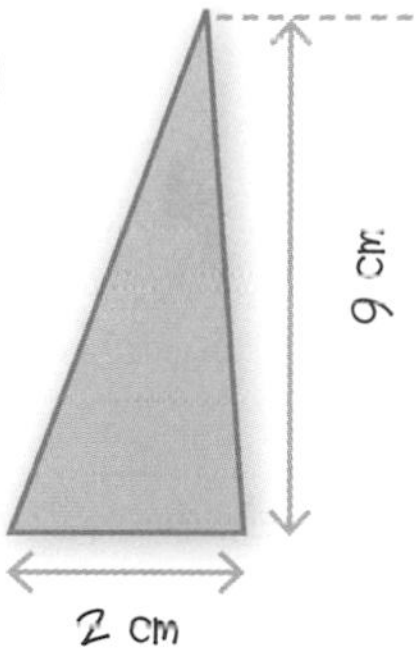

**b)**
4 cm
6 cm

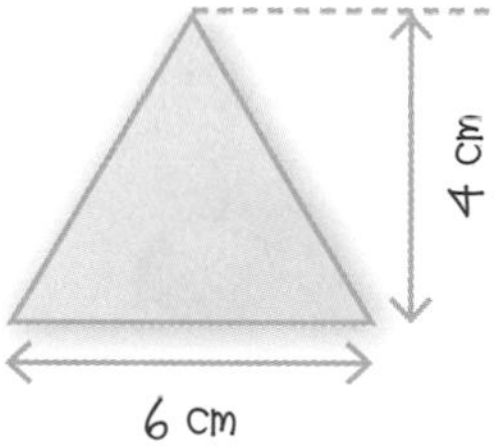

**d)**
9 cm
4 cm

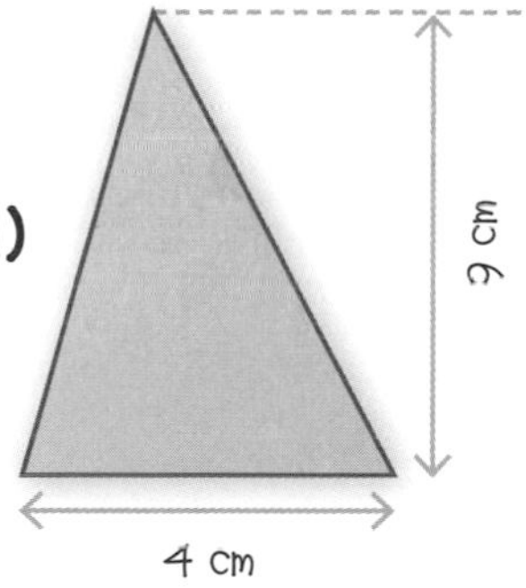

**f)**
5 cm
3 cm

**Challenge**

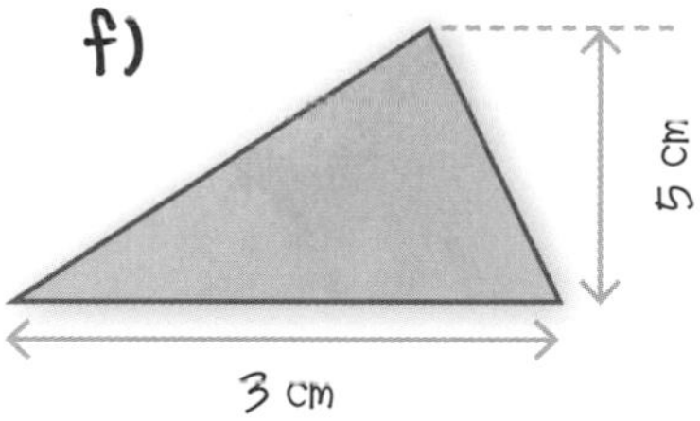

If each elephant shrew wants a piece of cheese 1 cm², how many shrews can this piece of cheese feed?

shrews

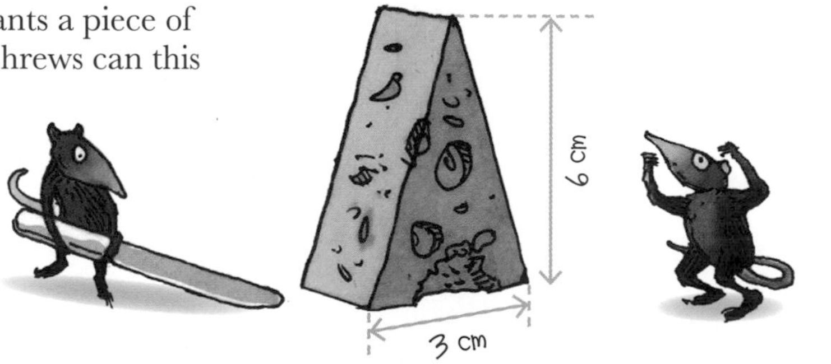

6 cm
3 cm

111

# Maps and coordinates

Maps are scaled-down versions of real places. They are divided into grids of equal-sized squares. These squares are labeled horizontally and vertically so that each can be identified by a letter and a number. These are written as coordinates in the order (letter, number).

Warm-up

The mammoths and elephant shrews have a map to show them how to find the biggest pumpkins. They need to avoid hazards such as the swamps, quarries, and murky lakes. Help them understand how to use a map by answering the questions.

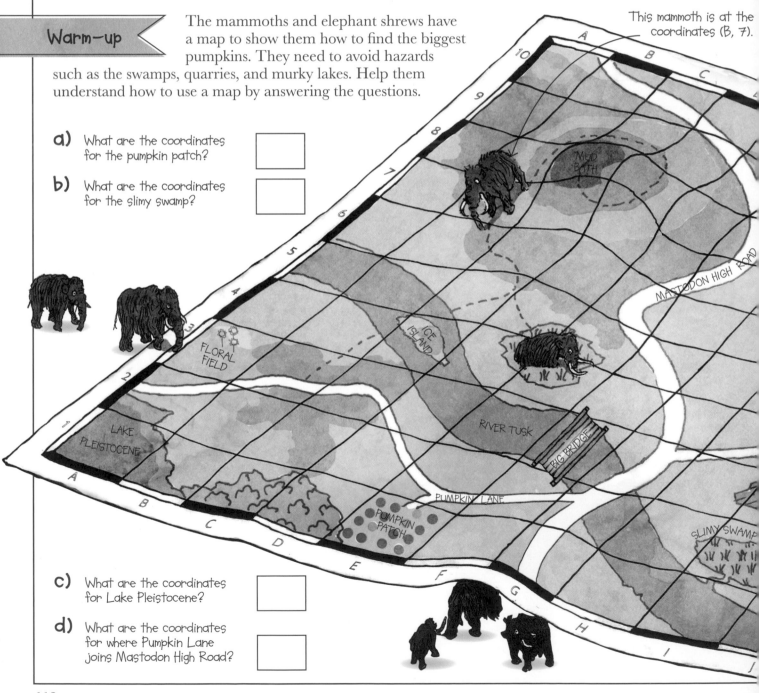

This mammoth is at the coordinates (B, 7).

a) What are the coordinates for the pumpkin patch?

b) What are the coordinates for the slimy swamp?

c) What are the coordinates for Lake Pleistocene?

d) What are the coordinates for where Pumpkin Lane joins Mastodon High Road?

## Reading coordinates

To find the coordinates of a square, first read the letter from the horizontal axis and then the number from the vertical axis.

Halfway between the points are northeast, southeast, southwest, and northwest.

## Using a compass

A compass shows directions as angles, called bearings, measured clockwise from north (0°).

North

The needle on a compass points to the north.

East

West

South

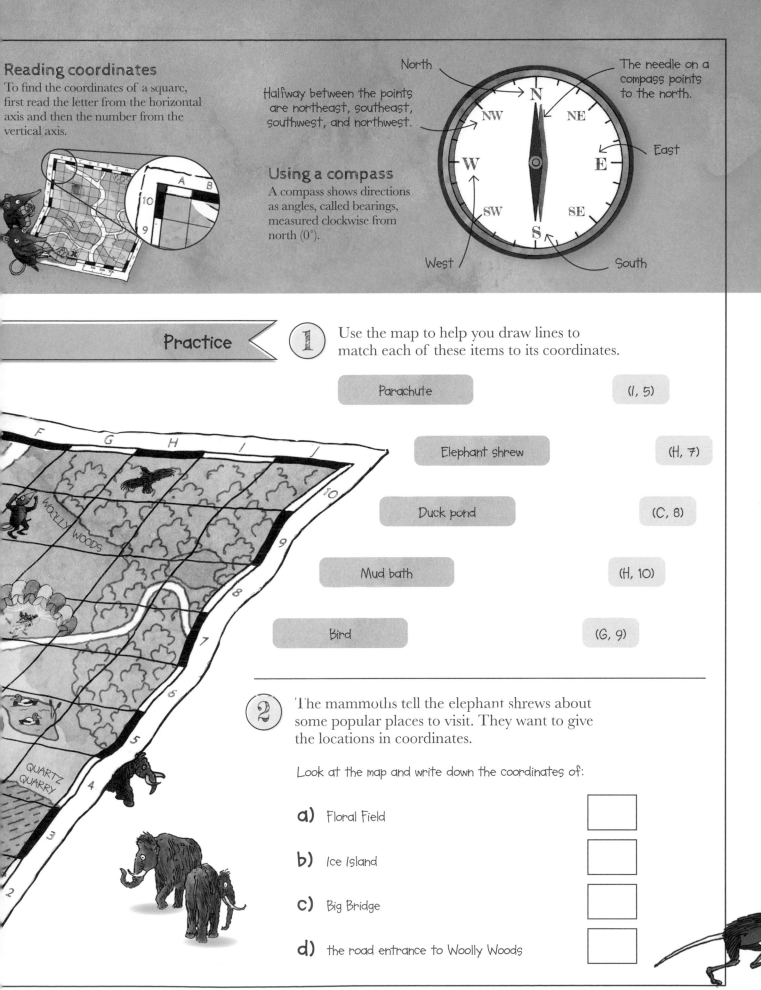

### Practice

**1** Use the map to help you draw lines to match each of these items to its coordinates.

| Parachute | (I, 5) |
| Elephant shrew | (H, 7) |
| Duck pond | (C, 8) |
| Mud bath | (H, 10) |
| Bird | (G, 9) |

**2** The mammoths tell the elephant shrews about some popular places to visit. They want to give the locations in coordinates.

Look at the map and write down the coordinates of:

**a)** Floral Field

**b)** Ice Island

**c)** Big Bridge

**d)** the road entrance to Woolly Woods

**3** Draw lines to match each compass direction with where it should be on the compass dial. The first one has been done for you.

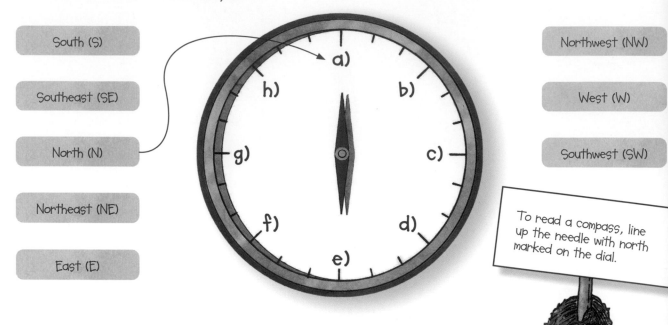

South (S)

Southeast (SE)

North (N)

Northeast (NE)

East (E)

Northwest (NW)

West (W)

Southwest (SW)

To read a compass, line up the needle with north marked on the dial.

**4** The mammoths are trying to reach the picnic paddock, but some of their directions are missing. Fill in the missing compass directions to get them to the paddock.

**a)** From the starting point, travel _____ until you reach the giant tree.

**b)** Then go _____ until you reach the river.

**c)** Turn _____ to cross the river over the bridge.

**d)** Finally, go _____ until you see the flag in the picnic paddock.

Picnic paddock

Starting point

5 The mammoths have chosen pumpkins for each elephant shrew and given them directions from the entrance to find the right one. Write in the coordinates of each pumpkin. The first one has been done for you.

a) 2 squares west          (C, 4)

b) 4 squares west, then 3 squares south

c) 3 squares west, then 1 square north

d) 2 squares west, then 2 squares south

Entrance

Challenge

Some elephant shrews are traveling around Mammoth Island. Look at the map and answer the questions.

a) An elephant shrew starts at Acorn Village, travels 7 squares north, then 1 square west. What place does it land? _____

b) An elephant shrew starts at Lake Splendid, travels 9 squares east, then 4 squares south. What place does it land? _____

c) An elephant shrew starts at Crow City, travels 6 squares west, then 3 squares north. What coordinates does it land at?

d) An elephant shrew starts at Evergreen Forest, travels 2 squares north, 3 squares west, then 3 squares south. What coordinates does it land at?

115

# Volume

Volume tells us the amount of space something takes up in a 3D shape or container. We measure the volume of liquids and solids using different units.

Warm-up

The elephant shrews want to know the volume of a box. They have filled the box with neat rows of sugar cubes, then taken the big box away so they can see the cubes.

**a)** What is the height of the cube of sugar lumps?  ☐

**b)** What is the length of the cube of sugar lumps?  ☐

**c)** What is the width of the cube of sugar lumps?  ☐

**d)** What is the volume of the box?

☐ × ☐ × ☐ = ☐ cm³

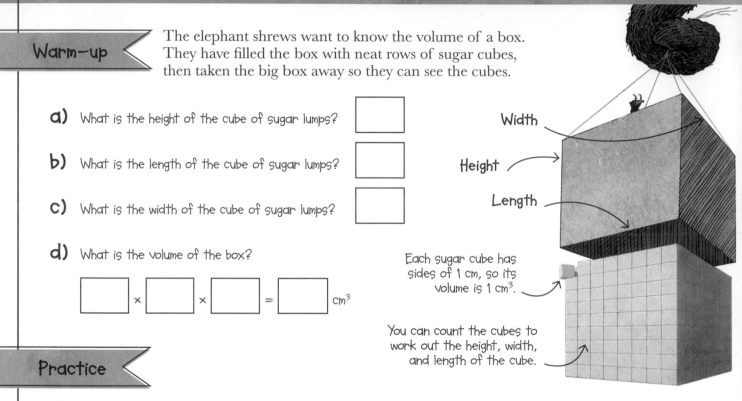

Width

Height

Length

Each sugar cube has sides of 1 cm, so its volume is 1 cm³.

You can count the cubes to work out the height, width, and length of the cube.

Practice

**1** Count the cubes to work out the volume of these shapes.

**a)**
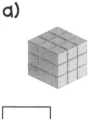
☐ cubes

**b)**
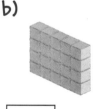
☐ cubes

**c)**
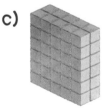
☐ cubes

**d)**

☐ cubes

**e)**

☐ cubes

**2** For each measuring cup, give the volume shown in milliliters. The first one has been done for you.

**a)**
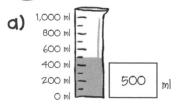
1,000 ml
800 ml
600 ml
400 ml
200 ml
0 ml
500 ml

**b)**
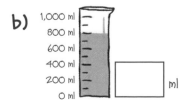
1,000 ml
800 ml
600 ml
400 ml
200 ml
0 ml
☐ ml

**c)**
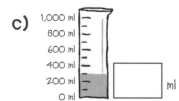
1,000 ml
800 ml
600 ml
400 ml
200 ml
0 ml
☐ ml

1,000 ml = 1 liter
So 500 ml = 0.5 liters (1/2 liter)

## Solids

Volume of solids is measured using cubic units. Each unit has exactly the same measurements for length, width, and height. We show cubic units with a little 3, like this: 1 cm³.

Each side of this cube measures 1 cm, which gives the cube a volume of 1 cm³.

## Liquids

Liquid volume is measured in liters and milliliters (ml).

## Calculating volume

There are two ways to find the volume of something solid. We can either count cubes or we can use this formula:

Volume = Length × Width × Height

---

 **3** Draw lines to match the 3D shape to its volume.

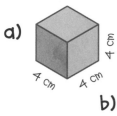

a)
4 cm
4 cm
4 cm

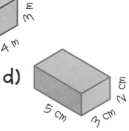

c)
5 m
4 m
3 m

b)
6 km
4 km
3 km

d)
5 cm
3 cm
2 cm

 60 m³

 72 km³

 30 cm³

 64 cm³

---

 **4** Complete the number sentences to find the volume.

a) 4 cm × 5 cm × 6 cm = [    ] cm³

b) 40 mm × 30 mm × 50 mm = [    ] mm³

c) 2 cm × 3 cm × 7 cm = [    ] cm³

d) 3 m × 4 m × 10 m = [    ] m³

e) 3 km × 2 km × 12 km = [    ] km³

f) 3 mm × 2 mm × 9 mm = [    ] mm³

---

 **5** Use the formula for finding the volume of a cuboid to calculate these volumes.

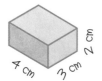
4 cm
3 cm
2 cm

a) [    ] cm³

8 mm
8 mm
8 mm

b) [    ] mm³

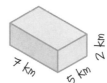
7 km
5 km
2 km

c) [    ] km³

---

**Challenge**

A mammoth has watered some vegetables with 1,250 ml of water from a watering can that holds 3 liters.

How much is left to water the flowers in the next bed? [    ] ml

# Speed

Speed measures how far something travels in a certain amount of time. Speed is a compound measurement, which means it involves two or more measurements.

$$\text{Speed} = \frac{\text{Distance}}{\text{Time}}$$

The elephant shrews want to know how fast the mammoth can run. They use a stopwatch and time how long it takes the mammoth to run 100 meters.

**a)** What distance did the mammoth run? ☐ meters

**b)** How long did it take to run that distance? ☐ seconds

**c)** What was the mammoth's speed?

$$\frac{\boxed{\phantom{00}} \text{ m}}{\boxed{\phantom{00}} \text{ s}} = \boxed{\phantom{00}} \text{ m/s}$$

*100 m*

m/s means meters per second

(1) Use the formula triangles to help you work out the speed or time.

**a)** The speed of an elephant shrew who runs 50 meters in 10 seconds.

☐ m/s

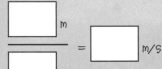
*50 m | 10 s*

**b)** How long it would take a mammoth running at 60 km/h to run 360 km.

☐ h

*360 km | 60 km/h*

**c)** How long it takes a mammoth walking at 5 km/h to walk a distance of 30 km.

☐ h

*30 km | 5 km/h*

**d)** The speed of a mammoth who runs 400 m in 50 seconds.

☐ m/s

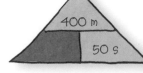
*400 m | 50 s*

## Formula triangle

Using a formula triangle helps work out one of the values if you know the value of the other two.

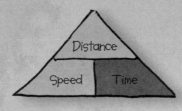
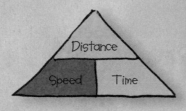
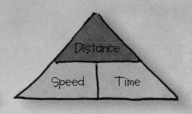

$$Speed = \frac{Distance}{Time}$$

$$Time = \frac{Distance}{Speed}$$

$$Distance = Speed \times Time$$

---

**2** An elephant shrew runs across a park. The distance is 80 meters. The shrew takes 16 seconds to cross the park.

What is the shrew's speed? ☐ m/s

**3** A mammoth walks at 4 kilometers per hour.

How long does it take the mammoth to walk a distance of 20 km? ☐ h

---

**4** A cheetah runs at 80 kilometers per hour.

How long would it take the cheetah to run 240 km? ☐ h

**5** A hippo covers a distance of 90 km in 3 hours.

What is its speed? ☐ km/h

---

**6** A race course is 1,200 m long. These animals take part in a race.

How much quicker does the cheetah complete the course than the other animals?

Cheetah: speed 25 m/s

Horse: speed 10 m/s

Cat: speed 8 m/s

**a)** The cheetah is ☐ s faster than the horse.

**b)** The cheetah is ☐ s faster than the cat.

---

 **Challenge**

One of the mammoths uses a stopwatch to time how quickly an elephant shrew can walk or run 5 meters. Use the information in the table to work out the speed the shrew was traveling.

| Time to walk the distance | Time to run the distance |
| --- | --- |
| 5 seconds | 2.5 seconds |

**a)** Walking speed: ☐ m/s

**b)** Running speed: ☐ m/s

119

# Weight and mass

Mass is the amount of matter or material inside an object and is measured in milligrams, grams, kilograms, and metric tons. Weight is the amount of gravity acting on an object and is measured in Newtons (N).

Warm-up

The elephant shrews are measuring their own mass and that of other animals.

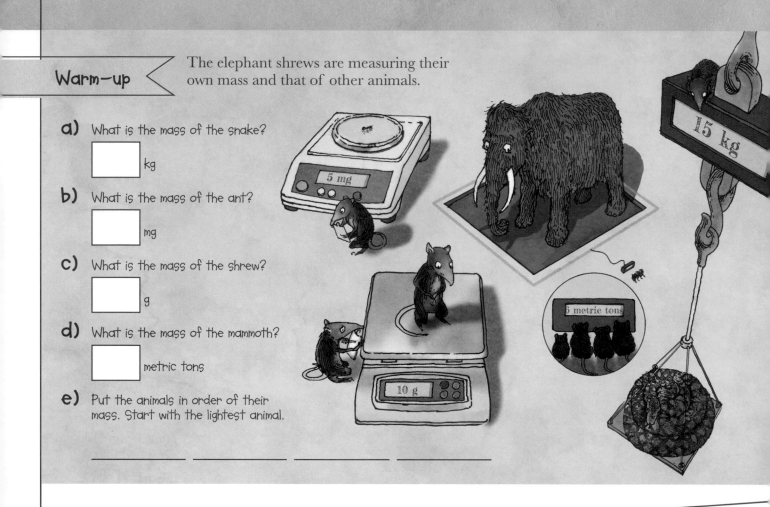

a) What is the mass of the snake?

☐ kg

b) What is the mass of the ant?

☐ mg

c) What is the mass of the shrew?

☐ g

d) What is the mass of the mammoth?

☐ metric tons

e) Put the animals in order of their mass. Start with the lightest animal.

_____ _____ _____ _____

## Practice

To convert between units:
Milligrams ÷ 1,000 = grams
Grams ÷ 1,000 = kilograms
Kilograms ÷ 1,000 = metric tons

1 Draw lines to match the same weights given in different units.

| 5 kg | 1 metric ton | 300,000 g | 200 mg |

| 1,000 kg | 0.2 g | 5,000 g | 3 metric tons |

**2** Use the words in the boxes to help you complete these sentences. You will need to use one word twice.

weight          mass

**a)** The _____ of the shrew is 98 N.

**b)** The _____ of the mammoth is 200,000 kg.

**c)** The _____ of the pigeon is 5 N.

**3** Put these animals in order from lightest to heaviest.

| Animal | Mass |
|--------|------|
| Cat | 5,250 g |
| Dog | 9.75 kg |
| Hamster | 180 g |
| Parrot | 0.54 kg |
| Rabbit | 2,400 g |

Lightest

a) _____
b) _____
c) _____
d) _____

Heaviest   e) _____

---

**4** Find the weight of each of the elephant shrews on Earth.

**a)** First, convert all the masses given into kilograms. The first one has been done for you.

**b)** Now convert the mass of each elephant shrew into its weight on Earth. The first one has been done for you

Weight on Earth (N)
= mass (kg) × 10

| Animal | Mass (g) | Mass (kg) |
|--------|----------|-----------|
| Shrew 1 | 10 | 0.01 |
| Shrew 2 | 6 | |
| Shrew 3 | 7.5 | |
| Shrew 4 | 28 | |
| Shrew 5 | 17 | |

| Animal | Weight on Earth (N) |
|--------|---------------------|
| Shrew 1 | 0.1 |
| Shrew 2 | |
| Shrew 3 | |
| Shrew 4 | |
| Shrew 5 | |

**Challenge**

Complete the table to show the weight of each animal on the Earth, then the weight on the Moon. For each animal, work out the difference between the weight on the Earth and the weight on the Moon.

To find the weight of anything on the Moon, we multiply its mass in kg by 1.6.

| Animal | Mass on Earth (kg) | Weight on Earth (N) | Weight on Moon (N) | Difference (N) |
|--------|--------------------|--------------------|--------------------|----------------|
| Elephant shrew | 0.9 kg | | | |
| Mammoth | 5,500 kg | | | |
| Pigeon | 0.51 kg | | | |
| Snake | 15 kg | | | |

121

# Temperature

Temperature is a measure of how hot or cold something is. We measure temperature using thermometers. A thermometer contains a colored liquid that expands when it is hot and contracts when it is cold. As the liquid expands and contracts, it moves up and down the scale, telling us the temperature.

### Different scales

The scale on the side allows us to read the temperature in different units: degrees Fahrenheit (°F) and degrees Celsius (°C).

68°F (20°C) is a comfortable room temperature.

32°F (0°C) is the freezing point of water.

Temperatures can go into negative figures, too.

Warm-up

The mammoths are using thermometers to measure temperature. Circle the thermometers that show temperatures above 50°F (10°C).

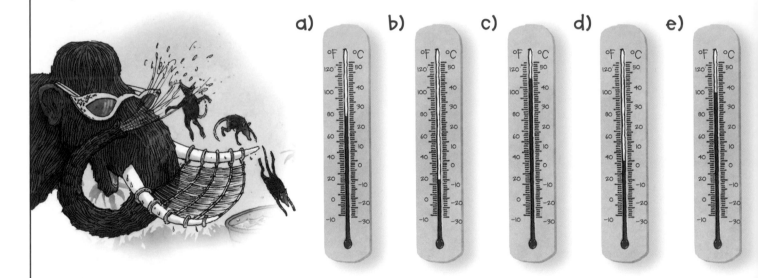

a)    b)    c)    d)    e)

Practice

 Draw lines to match the correct temperatures for each of these pictures.

Room temperature

Boiling water

Ice cubes

32°F

68°F

212°F

**2** On each of the thermometers, color in the scale to show the correct temperature.

**a)** 10°C

**b)** −5°F

**c)** −20°C

**d)** 100°F

**3** The elephant shrews have researched some high temperatures recorded in different countries.

| Country | Temperature (°F) |
|---|---|
| Germany | 104.9 |
| Greenland | 74.5 |
| Brazil | 112.6 |
| Antarctica | 67.6 |
| Australia | 123.3 |
| Finland | 98.9 |
| Japan | 105.9 |

Put the countries in order of temperature. Start with the coolest.

a) _____     e) _____

b) _____     f) _____

c) _____     g) _____

d) _____

**4** The elephant shrews are taking the temperature of a group of children, to check whether they have a fever. Normal body temperature is 98.6°F and a reading of 100.4°F and above is a fever.

Circle the patients that should be treated for a fever.

| Patient | Temperature (°F) |
|---|---|
| Leah | 98.6 |
| Theo | 98.2 |
| Almut | 100.8 |
| Siobhan | 98.4 |
| Mia | 100.4 |
| Apeksha | 100.2 |
| Lucas | 98.0 |

**Challenge**

Thermometers come in different shapes and sizes. The elephant shrews have found two different thermometers, each showing a different temperature.

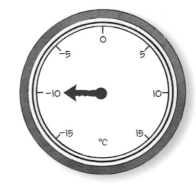

What is the difference between the two temperatures?

[ ] °F

123

# Telling time

Measuring the time helps us keep track of things, like how long to bake a cake or how long a journey may take. We use a clock to tell time and we measure time in hours, minutes, and seconds.

**Analog clock**

The short hand shows the hour.

The long hand shows minutes.

## Types of clocks
Analog clocks have hands that move around a circular face. Digital clocks show the time using numbers on a display.

**Digital clock**

Some digital clocks display all 24 hours in a day, starting from midnight (00:00).

> **Warm-up**

The mammoths have made a giant clock. Help them understand it by filling in the blanks. The first one has been done for you.

There are 24 hours in one day: 12 hours between midnight and noon, and another 12 between noon and midnight.

There are __24__ hours in 1 day, but only _____ hours on an analog clock.

When the short hand points up at _____, it is either midday or _____.

The short hand goes all the way around the clock twice in _____ day.

There are _____ minutes in 1 hour.

There are _____ seconds in 1 minute.

> **Practice**

**1** Shade the clock faces to show how many hours have passed since 12 o'clock. The first one has been done for you.

a)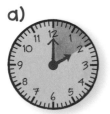
2 o'clock

b)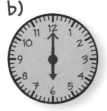
6 o'clock

c)
10 o'clock

**2** Shade the clock faces to show how many minutes after the hour. The first one has been done for you.

a)
5 after 4

b)
quarter after 10

c)
half past 2

124

## Clock hands

We can read what time it is on an analog clock by looking at where each hand is pointing.

When the long hand points at 12, it is the start of a new hour. This clock shows 2 o'clock.

When the long hand points at 6, it is halfway through the hour. This clock shows half past 2.

When the long hand points at 3, it is a quarter of the way through the hour. This clock shows quarter after 2.

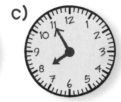

When the long hand points at 9, it is three-quarters of the way through the hour, or a quarter until the next hour. This clock shows quarter to 3.

---

**(3)** Shade the clock faces to show how many minutes left until the next hour. The first one has been done for you.

**a)**     **b)**     **c)** 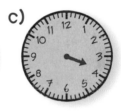    **d)**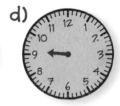

25 to 5          quarter to 7          5 to 8          half past 6

---

**(4)** Draw the missing minute hand on each clock to show the time written below it.

**a)**     **b)** 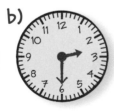    **c)**     **d)**

8 o'clock          quarter after 5          quarter to 4          10 after 9

---

**(5)** Draw lines to match each clock face with the digital clock showing the same time.

**a)** **b)** **c)** **d)** **e)** **f)**

10:15

 6:45     4:05     8:00     4:35     2:30

**6** The elephant shrews were supposed to take their pies out of the oven at 3 o'clock.
Fill in the digital clocks to show what time each pie came out of the oven.

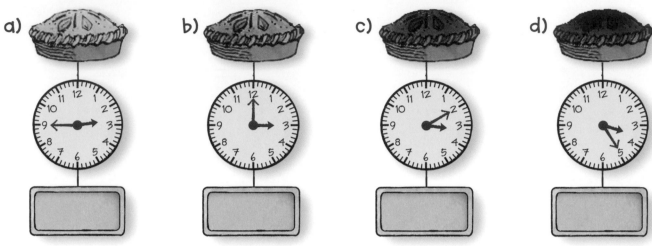

a)

b)

c)

d)

**7** Draw lines to match each 12-hour digital clock with the 24-hour clock showing the same time.
The first one has been done for you.

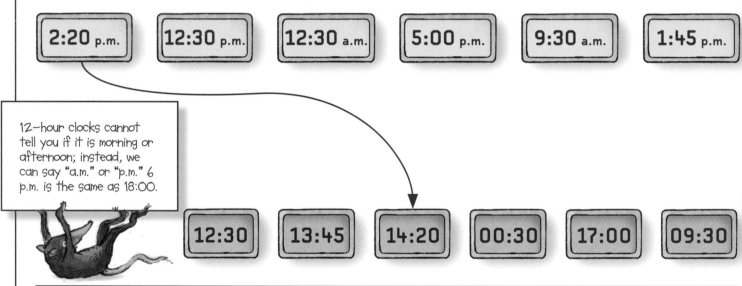

| 2:20 p.m. | 12:30 p.m. | 12:30 a.m. | 5:00 p.m. | 9:30 a.m. | 1:45 p.m. |

12-hour clocks cannot tell you if it is morning or afternoon; instead, we can say "a.m." or "p.m." 6 p.m. is the same as 18:00.

| 12:30 | 13:45 | 14:20 | 00:30 | 17:00 | 09:30 |

**8** Draw hands on each analog clock to show the same time as each 24-hour digital clock.

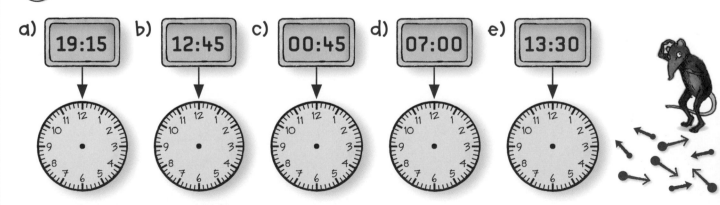

a) 19:15    b) 12:45    c) 00:45    d) 07:00    e) 13:30

**9** Put the clocks in order of time. Number them from 1 for the earliest to 5 for the latest time.

a)

|  |  |  |  |  |
|---|---|---|---|---|

b)

| 02:50 | 20:15 | 00:40 | 23:55 | 15:05 |
|---|---|---|---|---|

---

Challenge

The mammoths had a long-distance running race. The elephant shrews timed them but had to use different clocks. Use the start and finish times to work out the time each mammoth took to run the race. Circle the number of the mammoth who finished first.

| Mammoth | Start time | Finish time | Time taken in hours and minutes |
|---|---|---|---|
| 1 | 13:30 | 14:30 | |
| 2 | | | |
| 3 | 1:30 p.m. | 2:15 p.m. | |
| 4 | 13:30 | 14:25 | |
| 5 | | | |

127

# Gathering data

"Data" is another word for "information." There are different ways of collecting data, including making and recording observations and carrying out surveys. The type of mathematics that deals with collecting, organizing, and analyzing data is called statistics.

**Warm-up**

The mammoths are collecting data on the number of birds that visit their garden during the week. Can you help them by drawing tally marks on the clipboard for the birds that visited in one day? The first one has been done for you.

**Practice**

1. Help the elephant shrews match the tally marks with the correct number.

a) |||| |||| |       29

b) |||| |||| |||| |||| |||| ||       18

c) |||| |||| |||| |||| |||| ||||       11

d) |||| |||| |||| |||       27

## Tally marks

Tally marks can be used to count quickly when collecting data. By grouping tally marks in sets of 5, it is easy to count up quickly and see patterns of numbers at a glance.

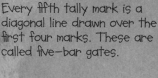

Every line is a "tally" mark. Each vertical line represents one thing.

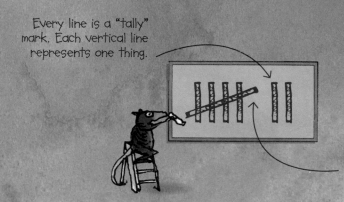

Every fifth tally mark is a diagonal line drawn over the first four marks. These are called five-bar gates.

**2** The elephant shrews did a survey of the birds at the bird feeder at different times of day.

Shrew 1 counted 1 magpie, 3 sparrows, and 3 pigeons.

Shrew 2 counted 2 finches, 4 sparrows, and 6 pigeons.

Shrew 3 counted 1 crow, 1 magpie, and 7 pigeons.

**a)** Use tally marks to record the results, then add them up to give the total number. The first column has been done for you.

|  | Magpie | Finch | Sparrow | Pigeon | Crow |
|---|---|---|---|---|---|
| Shrew 1 | I |  |  |  |  |
| Shrew 2 |  |  |  |  |  |
| Shrew 3 | I |  |  |  |  |
| Total number | II |  |  |  |  |

**b)** Which bird was seen the most often? _____

---

**Challenge**

Collect some data about the birds you see in your own garden or a park you visit. Use the blank table below to record your data.

**a)** Record your data using tally marks in this table. You might want to watch the birds for a little while before you start recording your data. Then you will know which birds to record in the columns.

|  |  |  |  |  |  |
|---|---|---|---|---|---|
| Number of birds |  |  |  |  |  |

**b)** Which bird did you see the most of? _____

# Graphs and charts

Once you have collected your data, there are lots of ways to present it. Charts and graphs are useful to understand data in a visual way. There are different charts that you can use depending on the data you want to present.

**Presenting data**
A bar chart uses columns or bars to show data. A line graph is a useful way to show how data changes over time. A pie chart shows how different subsets of data compare to each other.

**Warm-up**

The elephant shrews collected data about the birds at the feeding table, then drew a bar chart to display the data. Use the chart to answer these questions.

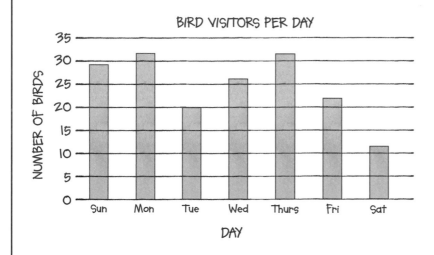

BIRD VISITORS PER DAY

**a)** On which day did the shrews see the fewest birds? _____

**b)** How many birds visited on Tuesday? _____

**c)** On how many days did the shrews see more than 25 birds? _____

**Practice**

**1** The mammoths collected data about birds that visited their garden as well. Use the bar chart to complete the frequency table.

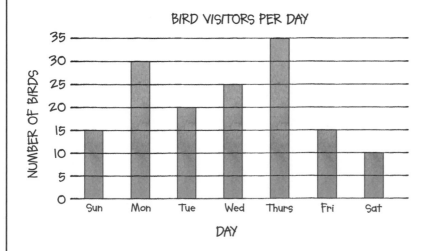

BIRD VISITORS PER DAY

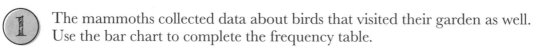

| Day | Number of birds |
| --- | --- |
| Sunday | |
| Monday | |
| Tuesday | |
| Wednesday | |
| Thursday | |
| Friday | |
| Saturday | |

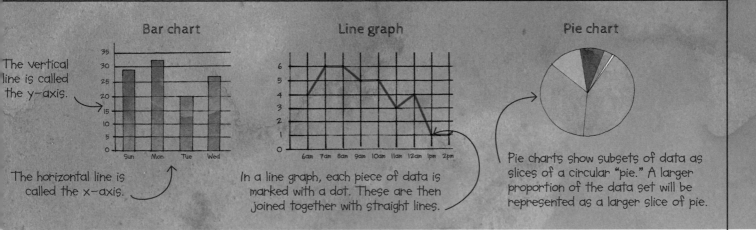

**Bar chart**

The vertical line is called the y-axis.

The horizontal line is called the x-axis.

**Line graph**

In a line graph, each piece of data is marked with a dot. These are then joined together with straight lines.

**Pie chart**

Pie charts show subsets of data as slices of a circular "pie." A larger proportion of the data set will be represented as a larger slice of pie.

---

**2** Two elephant shrews counted the types of birds that had visited the garden in one day. Use the frequency table to help you fill in the missing parts of the bar chart.

| Bird types | Number |
|---|---|
| Pigeons | 25 |
| Sparrows | 15 |
| Finches | 5 |
| Crows | 10 |
| Magpies | 2 |
| Unknown | 1 |

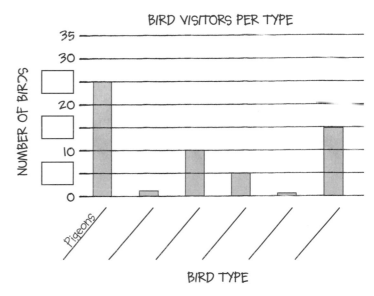

BIRD VISITORS PER TYPE

NUMBER OF BIRDS

BIRD TYPE

---

**3** The elephant shrews are looking at some data about what time of day birds visited the mammoths' garden. The data is displayed in a line graph.

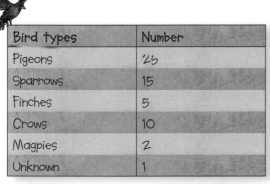

BIRD VISITORS PER HOUR

NUMBER OF BIRDS

TIME

**a)** How many birds visited at 6 a.m.?

**b)** How many birds visited at 4 p.m.?

**c)** When did the highest number of birds visit the garden?

**d)** What was the smallest number of birds to visit the garden?

131

**4** The mammoths have been recording the number of birds that visited every month for a year. The table shows the numbers they counted.

| Month | Jan | Feb | Mar | Apr | May | Jun | Jul | Aug | Sep | Oct | Nov | Dec |
|---|---|---|---|---|---|---|---|---|---|---|---|---|
| Number of birds | 200 | 200 | 250 | 250 | 350 | 200 | 400 | 350 | 700 | 600 | 500 | 300 |

The mammoths started making a line graph.

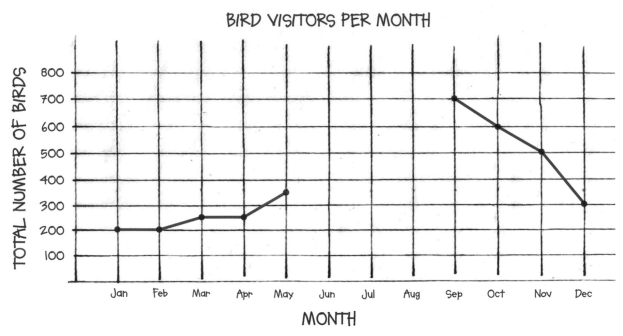

BIRD VISITORS PER MONTH

**a)** Complete the graph by plotting the points for June, July, and August and drawing the lines between the months with a ruler.

**b)** In which three months were the same number of birds counted? _____  _____ _____

**c)** What was the total number of birds that visited during October, November, and December? _____

---

**5** The elephant shrews recorded how many birds of each type visited the garden in a week and displayed the information in a pie chart.

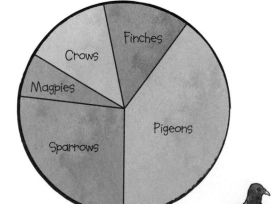

**a)** Which type of bird visited most frequently?

_____

**b)** Which type of bird visited least frequently?

_____

**c)** The total number of birds that visited the garden is 100. Which type of bird visited 30 times?

_____

**6** A group of elephant shrews were asked to name their favorite bird. This information is given in the pie chart.

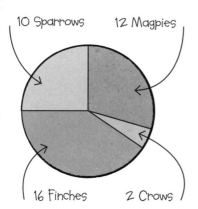

10 Sparrows    12 Magpies

16 Finches    2 Crows

Use the pie chart to fill in the missing information in the table. The first row has been done for you.

| | Number | Fraction | Percentage |
|---|---|---|---|
| Magpie | 12 | $^3/_{10}$ | 30% |
| Sparrow | | | |
| Finch | | | |
| Crow | | | |
| Total | | | |

The percentages shown in a pie chart always add up to 100.

---

**Challenge**

This pie chart shows the favorite sports of 50 elephant shrews. Work out the number of shrews who prefer each activity listed in the table using the information in the pie chart. The first one has been done for you.

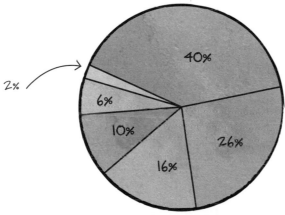

2%    6%    40%    10%    16%    26%

☐ Swimming
☐ Soccer
☐ Gym
☐ Dance
☐ Volleyball
☐ None

| Activity | Percentage | Number of shrews | |
|---|---|---|---|
| Swimming | 40% | 50 x 40 = 2,000 | 2,000 ÷ 100 = 20 shrews |
| Soccer | | | |
| Gym | | | |
| Dance | | | |
| Volleyball | | | |
| None | | | |

 You can check that your answers are practical by making sure that the percentage column adds up to 100 and the number of shrews column adds up to 50.

# Venn diagrams

In math, a set is a group of things or numbers that have something in common. By organizing sets into overlapping circles, Venn diagrams show you which members of a group are similar and which are different.

Warm-up

The mammoth has blown the whistle to tell the elephant shrews to get into different sets depending on which activity they enjoy. Those that enjoy more than one activity are in more than one set. Help the mammoth work out how many shrews belong to each set by filling in the blanks below.

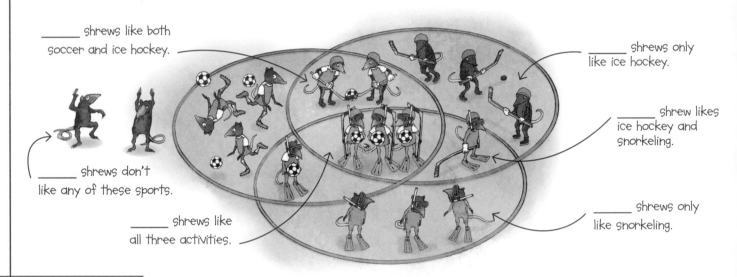

_____ shrews like both soccer and ice hockey.

_____ shrews only like ice hockey.

_____ shrew likes ice hockey and snorkeling.

_____ shrews don't like any of these sports.

_____ shrews like all three activities.

_____ shrews only like snorkeling.

Practice

**1** Look at this Venn diagram about the favorite hobbies of some other elephant shrews and answer the questions below.

a) How many shrews like swimming only?

b) How many shrews like hockey and running?

c) How many shrews are there in the whole group?

d) How many shrews like more than one activity?

e) How many shrews only like one activity?

134

## Organizing sets

In a Venn diagram, data is sorted into overlapping circles. The overlap is called an intersection. Data in the intersection belongs to both sets. Data that is not part of any set can sit outside of the circles.

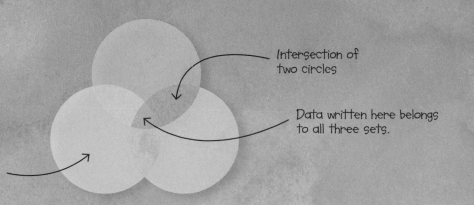

Intersection of two circles

Data written here belongs to all three sets.

Data in this part of the circle belongs only to this set.

---

**2** Add the numbers from the box into the correct place in this Venn diagram.

19   12   2   6

11   18   3

Even numbers

Prime numbers

---

**Challenge**

Here is information about the hobbies of some elephant shrews. Use the information in the table to put the shrews into the right places in the Venn diagram.

|  | Swims | Cannot swim |
|---|---|---|
| Plays soccer | Shrew 1<br>Shrew 2 | Shrew 5<br>Shrew 6 |
| Does not play soccer | Shrew 3<br>Shrew 4 | Shrew 7<br>Shrew 8 |

Swims

Plays soccer

# Averages

An average is a type of "middle" value that can be used to represent a set of data. Averages can be used to help compare data sets. There are three different types of averages: the mean, the median, and the mode.

The shrews represent a data set.

This group of mammoths are all different heights. The elephant shrews have measured each mammoth and want to use the data to calculate the mean, the median, the mode, and the range. Help the elephant shrews work out the different averages.

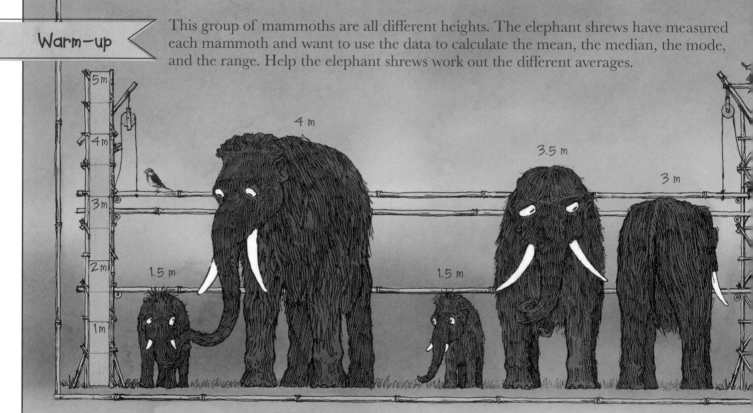

4 m

3.5 m

3 m

1.5 m

1.5 m

**a)** Fill in the blanks to help the elephant shrews work out the mean.

1.5 m + 4 m + 1.5 m + 3.5 m + 3 m = ☐ m

☐ ÷ 5 = ☐ m

**b)** What is the median height?

☐ ☐ ☐ ☐ ☐

Median = ☐ m

**c)** What is the mode? ☐ m

**d)** What is the range?

☐ m − ☐ m = ☐ m

Remember, to work out the median, put the heights in order first.

136

## The mean

The mean is the most commonly used average. It is the sum of all the values in a set, divided by the number of values. The mean of the shrew data set is:

$$\frac{8 + 8 + 8 + 10 + 10 + 10 + 9 + 9 + 10 + 11 + 12}{11} = \frac{105}{11} = 9.54$$

## The mode

The mode is the most common value in a set. The mode in the shrew data set is 10, as there are four number 10 shrews. There can be more than one mode for a set.

## The median

The median is the value that falls in the middle when all the values are placed in order. If we lined up all the shrews in order, it would look like this:

8  8  8  9  9  ⑩  10  10  10  11  12

↖ The median is 10.

## The range

The difference between the largest and smallest values in the set is called the range. The smallest value in our set is 8 and the largest is 12, so the range is 4.

## Practice

① The mammoths have collected some data about rainfall for five places on Mammoth Island.

| Place | April (cm) | May (cm) | June (cm) | July (cm) | August (cm) |
|---|---|---|---|---|---|
| Acorn Village | 15 | 6 | 5 | 5 | 2 |
| Crow City | 9 | 6 | 4 | 5 | 5 |
| Lake Splendid | 20 | 13 | 11 | 8 | 8 |
| Swamptown | 8 | 10 | 3 | 1 | 8 |
| Windy Bay | 3 | 2 | 2 | 6 | 0 |

a) What is the mean rainfall for Acorn Village? ☐ cm

b) What is the mean rainfall for Windy Bay? ☐ cm

c) Which place has the lowest mean rainfall? _____

d) Which place has the highest mean rainfall? _____

e) What is the median rainfall for Crow City? ☐ cm

f) What is the median rainfall for Swamptown? ☐ cm

g) What is the median rainfall for the whole island? ☐ cm

h) What is the mode for Acorn Village? ☐ cm

i) What are the modes for the whole island? ☐ cm ☐ cm

j) What is the range of rainfall in Lake Splendid? ☐ cm

k) What is the range of rainfall in Crow City? ☐ cm

137

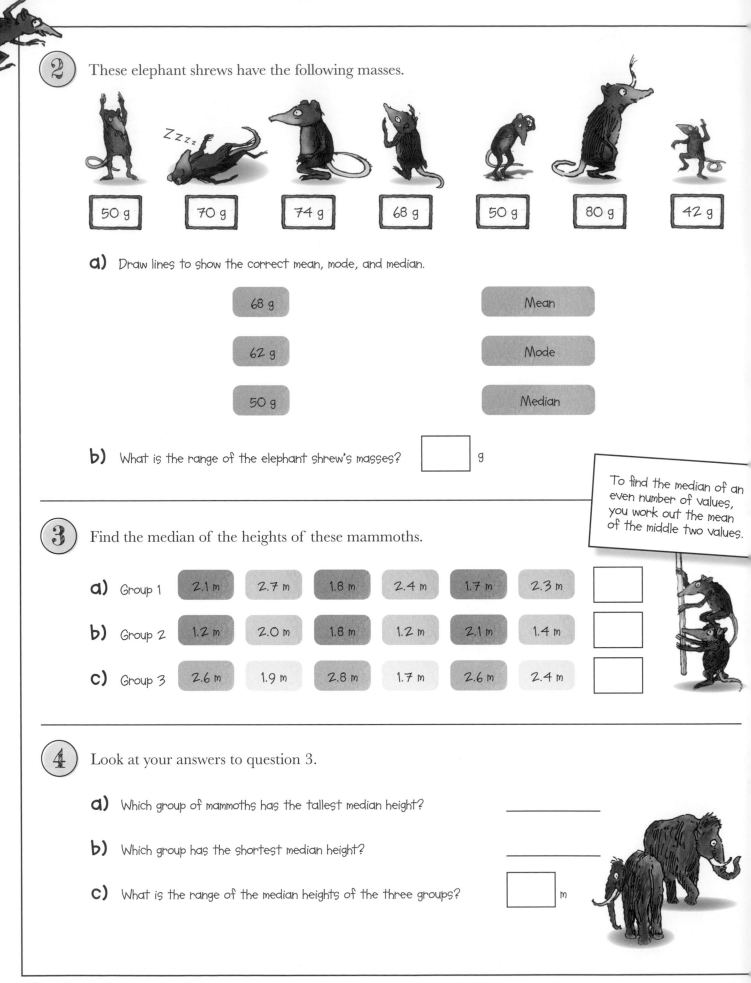

**2** These elephant shrews have the following masses.

50 g   70 g   74 g   68 g   50 g   80 g   42 g

**a)** Draw lines to show the correct mean, mode, and median.

68 g                    Mean

62 g                    Mode

50 g                    Median

**b)** What is the range of the elephant shrew's masses? [ ] g

> To find the median of an even number of values, you work out the mean of the middle two values.

**3** Find the median of the heights of these mammoths.

**a)** Group 1   2.1 m   2.7 m   1.8 m   2.4 m   1.7 m   2.3 m   [ ]

**b)** Group 2   1.2 m   2.0 m   1.8 m   1.2 m   2.1 m   1.4 m   [ ]

**c)** Group 3   2.6 m   1.9 m   2.8 m   1.7 m   2.6 m   2.4 m   [ ]

**4** Look at your answers to question 3.

**a)** Which group of mammoths has the tallest median height? _____

**b)** Which group has the shortest median height? _____

**c)** What is the range of the median heights of the three groups? [ ] m

138

**5** The elephant shrews recorded the number of birds they saw in their gardens on different days. Complete the table by identifying the mode or modes for each set.

| Day | Number of birds | Mode |
| --- | --- | --- |
| Monday | 10, 4, 4, 12, 3, 2, 7, 6 | |
| Tuesday | 10, 15, 4, 10, 18, 17, 15, 8, 7 | |
| Wednesday | 18, 7, 12, 10, 10, 16, 20, 21 | |
| Thursday | 12, 8, 7, 5, 5, 10, 16, 8 | |

**6** The elephant shrews have found out how much three items cost in five different stores.

| Food | Store 1 | Store 2 | Store 3 | Store 4 | Store 5 |
| --- | --- | --- | --- | --- | --- |
| Popcorn | $2.19 | $2.20 | $2.50 | $2.22 | $2.00 |
| Drink | 89¢ | $1.00 | $1.05 | 92¢ | 85¢ |
| Ice cream | $1.45 | $1.50 | $1.99 | $1.42 | $1.30 |

**a)** For each food, give the range.    Popcorn ☐   Drink ☐   Ice cream ☐

**b)** Which of the three foods has the largest range in price? Circle the correct answer.

    Popcorn       Drink       Ice cream

 Look at this data set, then answer these questions.

Challenge

   103   101   100   253   100   102   100   101

**a)** Most of the values are very close to each other, but one value is very different from the others. Identify the value.    ☐

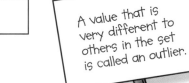

A value that is very different to others in the set is called an outlier.

**b)** Work out the value of the mean, median, and mode with this value included.

   Mean ☐   Median ☐   Mode ☐

**c)** Work out these averages again without the value included.

   Mean ☐   Median ☐   Mode ☐

**d)** What do you notice about the effect of this value on the averages? _____

# Probability

Probability describes how likely something is to happen. A high probability means something is more likely to happen. A low probability means it's unlikely to happen. We often use fractions to describe probability.

We can work out the probability of a shrew wearing a green hat using this formula:

$$\frac{\text{Number of shrews with green hats}}{\text{Total number of shrews}} = \frac{2}{6}$$

$\frac{2}{6}$ can be simplified to $\frac{1}{3}$. So, we can say that there's a 1 in 3 chance that a shrew will have a green hat.

**Warm-up**

The mammoths and elephant shrews are playing a party game. Help the mammoths understand what the probability is of catching the different shrews by filling in the blanks using the fractions given in the box.

$\frac{1}{2}$   $\frac{1}{4}$   $\frac{1}{12}$   $\frac{1}{6}$

**a)** The chance of catching a shrew with a yellow hat is 2/12, which can be simplified to _____ .

**b)** The chance of catching a shrew with a blue hat is _____ .

**c)** The chance of catching a shrew with a red hat is _____ .

**d)** The chance of catching a shrew with a green hat is _____ .

## Probability scale

All probabilities can be shown on a scale
according to how likely they are to happen.

**Definite**
The Sun always
rises. This event has
a probability of 1.

**Likely**
Things that probably
will happen are
higher up the scale.

**Even chance**
Things with an equal chance of
happening have a probability of
0.5. We can also write this as
½ or 50%.

**Unlikely**
Less likely things
are further down
the scale.

**Impossible**
At the bottom are
impossible events.
A mammoth growing wings
has a probability of 0.

1                                          0.5                                          0

## Practice

**1** Draw lines to match each event with the correct probability.

a) The number on a rolled die will be even.

b) There will be an elephant shrew in your house when you get home.

c) Rolling two dice will give a total of 2.

d) The day after Tuesday will be Wednesday.

e) Rolling two dice will give a total less than 10.

Definite

Likely

Equal chance

Unlikely

Impossible

**2** The elephant shrews have made this spinner to help them understand probability.

a) How many sections are there?

b) How many sections contain the number 1?

c) Use your answers to a) and b) to write
the fraction $b/a$.

d) Simplify your answer to c) to give the probability
of the spinner showing a 1.

e) What is the probability of the spinner showing a 2?

141

**3** The elephant shrews are carrying out a probability experiment with four orange, four purple, four red, and four white cards. They take turns selecting one at random.

1 2 3 4     1 2 3 4     1 2 3 4     1 2 3 4

Draw lines to match the card selections with how likely they are to happen.

◄ Definite    Likely    Equal chance    Unlikely    Impossible ►

A number greater than 4     A card with an odd number     A card that is not white

Purple number 4 card     A number less than 5

**4** The elephant shrews did a survey of some plants in different areas of a field and recorded their results on a clipboard.

|  | Area 1 | Area 2 | Area 3 |
|---|---|---|---|
| Dandelion | 4 | 2 | 2 |
| Daisy | 5 | 4 | 8 |
| Clover | 1 | 4 | 1 |
| Buttercup | 2 | 10 | 4 |
| Total | 12 | 20 | 15 |

**a)** What is the probability that a plant in area 2 is clover? Give your answer as a fraction.

**b)** What is the probability that a plant in area 1 is a daisy? Give your answer as a fraction.

**c)** In which area are you most likely to find a buttercup?

**5** Some elephant shrews voted for their favorite fruit. The total number of shrews who voted was 120. Here are the results.

| Fruit | Number of votes |
|---|---|
| Apple | 30 |
| Banana | 1 |
| Orange | 5 |
| Strawberry | 60 |
| Cherry | 24 |

**a)** What is the probability that a shrew voted for strawberry?

**b)** What is the probability that a shrew voted for apple?

**c)** What is the probability that a shrew voted for cherry?

**6** An elephant shrew rolls two dice and adds the scores up.
This grid shows some of the outcomes.

First dice

|   | 1 | 2 | 3 | 4 | 5 | 6 |
|---|---|---|---|---|---|---|
| 1 | 2 | 3 | 4 | 5 | 6 | 7 |
| 2 | 3 | 4 | __ | 6 | 7 | 8 |
| 3 | 4 | __ | 6 | __ | 8 | 9 |
| 4 | 5 | 6 | 7 | 8 | 9 | 10 |
| 5 | 6 | 7 | __ | 9 | 10 | 11 |
| 6 | __ | 8 | 9 | 10 | 11 | __ |

Second dice

**a)** Complete the table by writing the total scores in the empty boxes.

**b)** There are 36 different possible outcomes. What is the probability of an outcome with a total of 12?

_____

**c)** There are 6 different ways to get a total of 7. What is the probability of an outcome with this total?

_____

**d)** How many ways are there of getting an outcome with a total of 4?

_____

**e)** What is the probability of an outcome with a total of 4?

_____

**f)** The probability of an outcome with a total of 5 is $1/9$. What other total has the same probability?

_____

---

Challenge

The table shows the chance of snow on a day in December. Fill in the blank column with the probabilities shown as fractions.

"Chance" is the same as "probability."

| Time | Chance of snow | Probability of snow |
|---|---|---|
| 7 a.m. | 70% | |
| Noon | 95% | |
| 4 p.m. | 22% | |
| 9 p.m. | 52% | |

143

# Answers

## 6-7 Counting and number symbols

**Warm-up**

| | |
|---|---|
| 1—I | 6—VI |
| 2—II | 7—VII |
| 3—III | 8—VIII |
| 4—IV | 9—IX |
| 5—V | 10—X |

**Practice**

1  **a)** Number: 7, Roman numeral: VII
   **b)** Number: 4, Roman numeral: IV

2  **a)** 9   **b)** 3   **c)** 6

3  VII—7
   XXVIII—28
   CLXX—170
   DL—550

4  2016, 2007

**Challenge**

Learner's own answers.

## 8-9 Zero

**Warm-up**

1 mammoth + 0 mammoths = 1 mammoth
1 mammoth − 0 mammoths = 1 mammoth
1 mammoth × 0 mammoths = 0 mammoths

**Practice**

1  **a)** 3   **b)** 7   **c)** 50   **d)** 550   **e)** 5   **f)** 17   **g)** 58   **h)** 475

2  **a)** 0   **b)** 0   **c)** 0   **d)** 0

3  **a)** 132   **b)** 482   **c)** 1,065   **d)** 265   **e)** 356   **f)** 672

4  **b)** 435   **c)** 597   **d)** 832

5  **b)** 0   **c)** 0   **d)** 0

**Challenge**

**a)** 10°   **b)** −5°

## 10-13 Place value

**Warm-up**

1 pallet, 4 trays, 5 tubes, and 3 single apples have been packed. The total is 1,453.

**Practice**

1  **a)** 41   **b)** 63   **c)** 25   **d)** 437   **e)** 333   **f)** 1,841
   **g)** 1,682

2  5,793—3 ones
   3,975—3 thousands
   9,537—3 tens
   7,395—3 hundreds

3  1, 5, 0

4  **b)** Learner circles 9.
   **c)** Learner circles 0.
   **d)** Learner circles 7.

5  **b)** 4   **c)** 40   **d)** 400

6  **b)** 6,509   **c)** 2,180   **d)** 3,074   **e)** 269   **f)** 8,400
   **g)** 715

7  390, 8,302, and 2,360

**Challenge**

**a)** 80   **b)** 8,000   **c)** 8

## 14-17 Ordering and comparing numbers

**Warm-up**

From highest to lowest: 36,004, 23,865, 15,004

**Practice**

1  **b)** >   **c)** <   **d)** >   **e)** <   **f)** =   **g)** >   **h)** <   **i)** >   **j)** =

2  **a)** 987   **b)** 360   **c)** 728   **d)** 532   **e)** 920   **f)** 313

3  **b)** 9   **c)** 0   **d)** 9

4  From smallest to largest:
   **a)** 378, 405, 592
   **b)** 1,378, 3,187, 7,813
   **c)** 13,692, 14,873, 17,841

5  From largest to smallest:
   **a)** 588, 575, 568, 565
   **b)** 734, 713, 238, 128
   **c)** 1,267, 1,245, 256, 127

6  From highest to lowest: Purple team, Blue team, Yellow team, Green team, Red team, Orange team

7  From nearest to furthest: 14 km, 102 km, 200 km, 1,040 km

**Challenge**

**a)** 10,999   **b)** 10,902   **c)** 12,001   **d)** 14,820

## 18-19 Rounding

**Warm-up**

**a)** The digits 1, 2, 3, and 4 round down.
**b)** 82 rounds down to 80.
**c)** 162 rounds down to 160.
**d)** The digits 5, 6, 7, 8, and 9 round up.
**e)** 26 rounds up to 30.
**f)** 349 rounds up to 350.

**Practice**

1  70

2  **a)** 60   **b)** 40   **c)** 30   **d)** 80

3  **a)** 235, 238, 242, 244, 239
   **b)** 1,998, 2,002, 1,996, 2,003

4  **a)** 100   **b)** 300   **c)** 200   **d)** 100

5  7,972 and 8,023

**Challenge**

**a)** 5,000   **b)** 5,000   **c)** 6,000

## 20-21 Estimating

**Warm-up**

There are 20 shrews in the front row.

$20 \times 5 = 100$

**Practice**

**1 a)** 150 **b)** 60 **c)** 90

**2 a)** 500 **b)** 150

**3**        **a)** 2,500 **b)** 4,500 **c)** 7,500 **d)** 9,500

**4 a)** \$2 **b)** \$1 **c)** \$1.50 **d)** \$2 + \$1 + \$1.50 = \$4.50

**5 a)** \$2.50 + \$2 = \$4.50 **b)** \$3 + \$1.50 = \$4.50

   **c)** \$2 + \$2 + \$2 = \$6

**Challenge**

\$2 + \$2 + \$2 + \$2 + \$2 + \$2 = \$12

## 22-25 Addition

**Warm-up**

$4 + 2 = 6$

**Practice**

**1 a)** 3 **b)** 7 **c)** 12

**2 a)** 17 **b)** 107

**3 a)** 13 **b)** 16 **c)** 18

**4 a)** 157 **b)** 162 **c)** 168

**5 a)** 9 **b)** 19 **c)** 13

**6**   11 + 5—16           17 + 5—22

     12 + 2—14           18 + 7—25

     16 + 8—24           22 + 5—27

     13 + 13—26

**7 a)** 1,216 **b)** 1,208 **c)** 1,214 **d)** 1,209 **e)** 1,206

   **f)** 1,215 **g)** 1,217 **h)** 1,219

**8 a)** 30 **b)** 60 **c)** 160 **d)** 200

**9 a)** 56 **b)** 46 **c)** 78 **d)** 100 **e)** 75 **f)** 88

**Challenge**

12 + 5 + 8 + 3 = 28

## 26-29 Subtraction

**Warm-up**

**a)** 4 **b)** 9 − 4 = 5 **c)** 4 **d)** 6 − 4 = 2

**Practice**

**1 a)** 3 **b)** 1 **c)** 4 **d)** 5

**2 a)** 5 **b)** 3 **c)** 4 **d)** 7 **e)** 8 **f)** 6

**3 a)** 7 **b)** 9 **c)** 3 **d)** 1 **e)** 4 **f)** 5

**4 a)** 17 **b)** 13 **c)** 11 **d)** 15 **e)** 10 **f)** 12

**5 a)** 162 **b)** 157 **c)** 162 **d)** 150 **e)** 164 **f)** 150

**6 a)** 1,216 **b)** 1,208 **c)** 1,214 **d)** 1,205 **e)** 1,204

   **f)** 1,213 **g)** 1,203 **h)** 1,206 **i)** 1,205 **j)** 1,206

   **k)** 1,202 **l)** 1,201 **m)** 1,203 **n)** 1,204

**7 a)** 58 **b)** 26 **c)** 13 **d)** 36 **e)** 55 **f)** 13 **g)** 62

   **h)** 9 **i)** 31 **j)** 15

**8 a)** 60 **b)** 80 **c)** 90 **d)** 50

**Challenge**

**a)** 92 − 13 = 79

**b)** 48 − 22 = 26

**c)** 64 − 16 = 48

**d)** 84 − 33 = 51

**e)** 57 − 18 = 39

**f)** 75 − 42 = 33

## 30-31 Number bonds

**Warm-up**

There are two equal groups of **5** shrews. There are **10** shrews in total.

A number sentence to show this number bond is 5 + **5** = **10**.

**Practice**

**1 a)** 6 + 4 = 10 **b)** 7 + 3 = 10

**2 a)** 14 + 6 = 20 **b)** 18 + 2 = 20

**3 a)** 8 **b)** 4 **c)** 6 **d)** 2 **e)** 9 **f)** 3

**4 a)** 7 **b)** 3 **c)** 8 **d)** 18 **e)** 15 **f)** 4

**5 a)** 10 **b)** 50 **c)** 80 **d)** 40 **e)** 30 **f)** 20

**Challenge**

28—72

24—76

47—53

52—48

12—88

## 32-33 Negative numbers

**Warm-up**

The missing floor number order is: −3, −1, 2.

**Practice**

**1 a)** −2 **b)** −4 **c)** −6 **d)** −3

**2 a)** −3, −2, 2 **b)** −6, −5, −2, 0 **c)** −2, 0, 1, 4

   **d)** −6, −5, −3, −1, 1

**3 a)** 5 **b)** 6 **c)** 4

**4 a)** 2 **b)** −4 **c)** 1 **d)** 0

**5** From smallest to largest: −8, −7, −5, −3, 1

**Challenge**

60°F

## 34-37 Multiplication

**Warm-up**

**a)** 1   **b)** 12   **c)** 2   **d)** 6   **e)** 3   **f)** 4

**Practice**

**1** $3 + 3 = 6, 3 \times 2 = 6$

**2** $5 + 5 = 10, 5 \times 2 = 10$

**3** $2 + 2 + 2 + 2 + 2 + 2 = 12, 2 \times 6 = 12$

**4** $4 + 4 + 4 = 12, 4 \times 3 = 12$

**5** $7 + 7 + 7 = 21, 7 \times 3 = 21$

**6** **b)** 28   **c)** 30

**7** **a)** $5 \times 5 = 25$   **b)** $9 \times 4 = 36$   **c)** $4 \times 6 = 24$

**8** **a)** $3 \times 9 = 27$   **b)** $11 \times 4 = 44$   **c)** $8 \times 9 = 72$
**d)** $10 \times 3 = 30$   **e)** $4 \times 2 = 8$   **f)** $5 \times 7 = 35$
**g)** $8 \times 8 = 64$   **h)** $12 \times 5 = 60$

**9** **a)** $13 \times 0 = 0$   **b)** $10 \times 7 = 70$   **c)** $2 \times 10 = 20$
**d)** $2 \times 8 = 16$   **e)** $4 \times 4 = 16$   **f)** $4 \times 12 = 48$
**g)** $6 \times 11 = 66$

**10** Learner completes the multiplication chart by adding the numbers in bold.

| × | 1 | 2 | 3 | 4 | 5 | 6 | 7 | 8 | 9 | 10 | 11 | 12 |
|---|---|---|---|---|---|---|---|---|---|----|----|----|
| 1 | 1 | 2 | 3 | 4 | 5 | 6 | 7 | **8** | 9 | 10 | 11 | **12** |
| 2 | 2 | 4 | 6 | **8** | 10 | 12 | 14 | 16 | **18** | 20 | 22 | 24 |
| 3 | 3 | 6 | 9 | **12** | **15** | 18 | **21** | 24 | **27** | 30 | **33** | 36 |
| 4 | **4** | 8 | **12** | 16 | 20 | **24** | 28 | **32** | 36 | **40** | 44 | **48** |
| 5 | 5 | **10** | 15 | **20** | **25** | 30 | 35 | **40** | 45 | **50** | **55** | **60** |
| 6 | **6** | 12 | 18 | **24** | **30** | 36 | 42 | **48** | 54 | 60 | **66** | 72 |
| 7 | 7 | **14** | 21 | 28 | **35** | 42 | 49 | 56 | **63** | **70** | **77** | 84 |
| 8 | 8 | 16 | **24** | **32** | 40 | 48 | **56** | **64** | 72 | 80 | **88** | 96 |
| 9 | 9 | 18 | **27** | **36** | 45 | 54 | 63 | 72 | **81** | **90** | 99 | 108 |
| 10 | **10** | **20** | 30 | 40 | **50** | 60 | **70** | **80** | **90** | 100 | **110** | **120** |
| 11 | 11 | **22** | **33** | 44 | **55** | **66** | **77** | 88 | **99** | **110** | **121** | 132 |
| 12 | 12 | **24** | 36 | **48** | 60 | **72** | **84** | **96** | 108 | **120** | **132** | **144** |

**Challenge**

The mammoth has the greatest number of candies.

## 38-41 Division

**Warm-up**

**a)** 3   **b)** No

**Practice**

**1** **a)** 5   **b)** 3   **c)** 7

**2** **b)** 3 groups, $6 \div 2 = 3$   **c)** 6 groups, $12 \div 2 = 6$

**3** **a)** 8   **b)** 4   **c)** 9

**4**
| | |
|---|---|
| $36 \div 9$—4 | $28 \div 4$—7 |
| $4 \div 2$—2 | $48 \div 8$—6 |
| $48 \div 6$—8 | $30 \div 6$—5 |
| $18 \div 2$—9 | $6 \div 6$—1 |
| $21 \div 7$—3 | |

**5** **b)** 7 r1   **c)** 2 r3   **d)** 3   **e)** 2 r3   **f)** 3

**6** **b)** 4   **c)** 5   **d)** 3

**7** **a)** 4   **b)** 5   **c)** 6   **d)** 4   **e)** 7   **f)** 5   **g)** 8   **h)** 8   **i)** 2

**8** **a)** 54, 9   **b)** 56, 7   **c)** 50, 10   **d)** 60, 10   **e)** 64, 8
**f)** 63, 9   **g)** 72, 9   **h)** 81, 9   **i)** 28, 7

**Challenge**

**a)** They need to buy 8 packs of goggles.

**b)** 2 pairs of goggles will be spare.

**c)** They need to buy 10 packs of swim rings.

**d)** There won't be any spare.

## 42-43 Factors

**Warm-up**

**1** group of **8** muffins.

**2** groups of **4** muffins.

The shrews have found that the factors of 8 are **1**, **2**, **4**, and **8**.

**Practice**

**1** **b)** $1 \times 26, 2 \times 13$   **c)** $1 \times 12, 2 \times 6, 3 \times 4$
**d)** $1 \times 32, 2 \times 16, 4 \times 8$

**2** **b)** 1, 2, 3, 6, 7, 14, 21, 42
**c)** 1, 2, 4, 5, 10, 20
**d)** 1, 2, 4, 8, 16
**e)** 1, 5, 7, 35
**f)** 1, 2, 3, 6, 9, 18, 27, 54

**3** 1, 2, 4, 8, 16

**Challenge**

**a)** 16   **b)** 6   **c)** 12   **d)** 8

## 44-45 Prime numbers

**Warm-up**

3, 5, 7

**Practice**

**1** Learner colors 11, 13, and 17.

**2** **a)** 2 and 37   **b)** 53 and 73   **c)** 41   **d)** 61 and 79

**3** b, c, and e are prime number sequences

**4** **b)** The factors of 42 are 2 and 21, and 21 breaks down to 7 and 3.
**c)** The factors of 24 are 2 and 12, and 12 breaks down to 2 and 6, and 6 breaks down to 2 and 3.
**d)** The factors of 36 are 2 and 18, and 18 breaks down to 2 and 9, and 9 breaks down to 3 and 3.

**Challenge**

1379

## 46-47 Square numbers

**Warm-up**
1, 4, 9, 16, 25

**Practice**
1

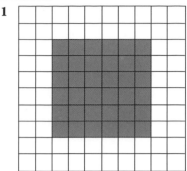

**2 b)** $15^2$ **c)** $36^2$ **d)** $67^2$ **e)** $8^2$ **f)** $91^2$

**3** Learner shades 64, 81, and 100.

**4** 52

**5** 9—3
16—4
25—5
4—2

**Challenge**
**a)** 7 **b)** 6 **c)** 9 **d)** 8 **e)** 11 **f)** 10

## 48-49 Cube numbers

**Warm-up**
**b)** $2^3$ **c)** $3^3$ **d)** $4^3$

**Practice**
**1 a)** $8^3$ **b)** $13^3$ **c)** $51^3$ **d)** $99^3$
**2** b
**3** 27
**4 a)** 125 **b)** 216
**5** 1, 8, 27, 64

**Challenge**
64

## 50-51 Magic shapes

**Warm-up**

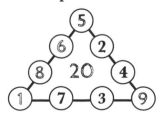

**Practice**
**1 a)**

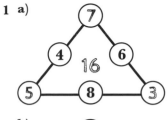

**d)**

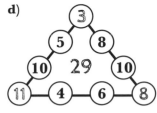

**b)**

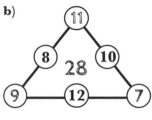

**e)**

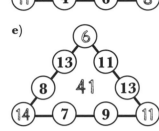

**c)**

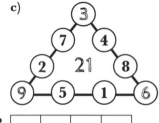

**2**

| 19 | 6 | **5** | 16 |
|----|----|----|----|
| **8** | 13 | 14 | 11 |
| 12 | **9** | 10 | 15 |
| 7 | 18 | 17 | **4** |

**3**

| 4 | **9** | 14 | 15 |
|----|----|----|----|
| 18 | 11 | **8** | 5 |
| 7 | 6 | 17 | **12** |
| **13** | 16 | 3 | 10 |

**Challenge**

| 27 | **7** | 5 | 33 |
|----|----|----|----|
| 17 | 21 | 23 | 11 |
| **25** | 13 | 15 | 19 |
| 3 | 31 | 29 | **9** |

The magic number is 72.

## 52-53 Equations

**Warm-up**

To find out how much the mammoth weighs, we put weights on the other side until the see-saw is **balanced**. This means that both sides of the see-saw are exactly the **same**.

When you see the **equals** sign, you know that the two sides must be balanced.

With four 1-ton weights on the side opposite to the mammoth, the see-saw balances. So we know that 1 mammoth = **4** tons.

**Practice**

**1** 3

**2 a)** 9  **b)** 16  **c)** 18  **d)** 5  **e)** 21  **f)** 37

**3 a)** 4  **b)** 3  **c)** 5  **d)** 4  **e)** 2  **f)** 4

**4 a)** 21  **b)** 35  **c)** 59  **d)** 77

**Challenge**

**a)** 11  **b)** 4  **c)** 8  **d)** 10

## 54-57 Fractions

**Warm-up**

**b)** $^4/_5$  **c)** $^3/_{10}$

**Practice**

**1 a)** ½  **b)** $^4/_8$  **c)** ¼  **d)** ¾  **e)** $^4/_6$  **f)** $^3/_8$

**2 b)**  **c)**  **d)**  **e)**
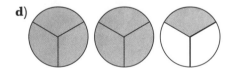

**3 b)** $^1/_3$  **c)** $^2/_5$  **d)** $^2/_8$  **e)** $^4/_6$  **f)** $^3/_7$

**4 a)** Learner circles 1 cupcake.
  **b)** Learner circles 4 cupcakes.
  **c)** Learner circles 5 cupcakes.

**5 b)** ½, ¾; Learner circles ¾.
  **c)** $^5/_{10}$, $^3/_{10}$; Learner circles $^5/_{10}$.
  **d)** $^1/_{10}$, $^6/_{10}$; Learner circles $^6/_{10}$.
  **e)** $^2/_3$, $^1/_3$; Learner circles $^2/_3$.
  **f)** $^1/_3$, ¼; Learner circles $^1/_3$.

**6**
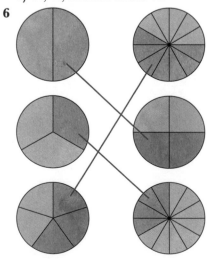

**7 a)**  **b)**  **c)**
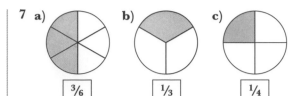

**Challenge**

3 slices are left, or $^3/_8$

## 58-59 Improper fractions and mixed numbers

**Warm-up**

Mixed numbers: $6^4/_5$, $4^1/_3$
Proper fractions: $^3/_5$, $^2/_7$
Improper fractions: $^7/_2$, $^{11}/_3$, $^{15}/_5$

**Practice**

**1 b)** $^5/_4$  **c)** $^7/_2$  **d)** $^{14}/_3$

**2 a)**
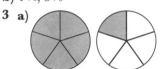

**b)** $1^3/_5$, $3^2/_5$

**3 a)**
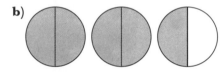

  **b)**

  **c)**

  **d)**
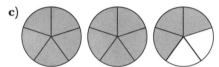

**4** $^{11}/_2$—$5\frac{1}{2}$
   $^9/_2$—$4\frac{1}{2}$
   $^{25}/_4$—$6\frac{1}{4}$
   $^{16}/_5$—$3\frac{1}{5}$
   $^{11}/_3$—$3\frac{2}{3}$
   $^{39}/_4$—$9\frac{3}{4}$
   $^{23}/_3$—$7\frac{2}{3}$
   $^8/_5$—$1\frac{3}{5}$

**5 a)** $5\frac{2}{3}$  **b)** $2\frac{2}{5}$

**6 a)** $^{13}/_3$  **b)** $^{19}/_8$

**Challenge**

25

## 60-61 Decimals

**Warm-up**

The order of 3rd prize to 1st prize is: 4.04 kg, 4.67 kg, 4.99 kg.

**Practice**

**1 b)** 0.3   **c)** 0.7   **d)** 0.6   **e)** 0.5

**2 b)** 0.03   **c)** 0.09   **d)** 0.12

**3** From smallest to largest: 0.02, 0.06, 0.07, 0.1, 0.4

**4** 0.7

**Challenge**

0.562—The largest number

0.43—The number has three hundredths

0.258—The smallest number

0.44—The tenths and hundredths digits are the same

## 62-63 Percentages

**Warm-up**

**a)** 50%   **b)** 25%   **c)** 24%   **d)** 25%

**Practice**

**1 a)** Learner colors 10 shrews blue.

  **b)** Learner colors 3 shrews green.

  **c)** Learner colors 6 shrews yellow.

  **d)** 30%

  **e)** 49%

  **f)** 51%

**2** 44% of the ice cream cones are blueberry.

**3 a)** 25%   **b)** 50%   **c)** 60%   **d)** 20%

**Challenge**

Nose: 20%, Middle: 40%, Base: 40%

## 64-65 Describing fractions

**Warm-up**

$1/5 = {}^2/_{10} = {}^{20}/_{100} = 20\% = 0.2$

$1/4 = {}^{25}/_{100} = 25\% = 0.25$

**Practice**

**1 a)** Learner shades 2 segments.

  **b)** Learner shades 5 segments.

  **c)** Learner shades 9 segments.

  **d)** Learner shades 3 segments.

  **e)** Learner shades 4 segments.

**2 a)** Learner shades 4 segments.

  **b)** Learner shades 5 segments.

  **c)** Learner shades 2 segments.

  **d)** Learner shades 1 segment.

  **e)** Learner shades 7 segments.

**3 a)** Learner shades 6 segments.

  **b)** Learner shades 3 segments.

  **c)** Learner shades 8 segments.

  **d)** Learner shades 9 segments.

  **e)** Learner shades 5 segments.

**4**

| Fraction | Decimal | Percentage |
| --- | --- | --- |
| $1/10$ | **0.1** | 10% |
| $1/2$ | 0.5 | **50%** |
| $2/10$ | 0.2 | 20% |
| $1/4$ | 0.25 | **25%** |
| $3/4$ | **0.75** | 75% |

**5** $0.5 - 1/2$

$^6/_{10} - 60\%$

$40\% - {}^4/_{10}$

$^7/_{10} - 0.7$

$0.8 - {}^4/_5$

**6** From smallest to largest: 10%, 0.2, ¼, 0.6, ¾

**Challenge**

From smallest to largest: 0.7, 1.3, 2½, 4¾, 540%

## 66-67 Ratio and proportion

**Warm-up**

**a)** 2:3   **b)** 5:3   **c)** 3:1   **d)** 3:4

**Practice**

**1 b)** 3:2   **c)** 4:1   **d)** 3:3

**2 a)** Red: $^4/_{10}$   **b)** Green: $^3/_{10}$   **c)** Blue: $^1/_{10}$   **d)** Black: $^2/_{10}$

**3 a)** $^3/_{12}$   **b)** $^5/_{12}$   **c)** $^2/_{12}$   **d)** $^1/_{12}$

**4 b)** $30 \div 100 = 0.3, 0.3 \times 200 = 60$

  **c)** $10 \div 100 = 0.1, 0.1 \times 200 = 20$

  **d)** $40 \div 100 = 0.4, 0.4 \times 200 = 80$

**Challenge**

**a)** 6   **b)** 3   **c)** 2

**d)** green paint $^6/_{18}$, red paint $^{12}/_{18}$

## 68-69 Scaling

**Warm-up**

b

**Practice**

**1 b)** $100 \div 300 = 0.3$   **c)** $150 \div 25 = 6$

**2 a)** Height = 2 m   **b)** Length = 4 m, Height = 1 m

**3 b)** $8 \times 10 \text{ m} = 80 \text{ m}$

  **c)** $6 \times 10 \text{ m} = 60 \text{ m}$

**Challenge**

Learner draws the original shape but double the size.

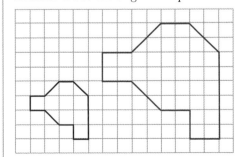

## 70-71 Sequences

**Warm-up**

The wool clothes make a sequence that goes like this: sock, **hat**, sock, mitten, mitten.

The sequence rule for these shirts is "take **three** away from each term to get the next term."

Numbers on the missing shirts are 5 and 2.

**Practice**

**1** Learner draws a mitten, then a sock, then a hat.

**2** Learner draws a triangle, then a square, then a pentagon.

**3**

**4 a)** 20, 22, 24   **b)** 10, 7, 4   **c)** 32, 64, 128   **d)** 10, 8, 5

**Challenge**

25, 36, 49

## 72-75 Angles

**Warm-up**

**a)** Acute   **b)** Right   **c)** Obtuse   **d)** Reflex

**Practice**

**1 b)** 0   **c)** 4   **d)** 2   **e)** 1

**2 a)** Learner colors in 1 segment.
   **b)** Learner colors in 1 segment.
   **c)** Learner colors in 2 adjoining segments.
   **d)** Learner colors in 1 segment.
   **e)** Learner colors in 3 adjoining segments.

**3** Learner colors in the angles shaded here:

**a)**    **b)**    **c)**

**4 b)** >   **c)** =   **d)** <   **e)** =   **f)** >

**5 b)** 70°, Acute   **c)** 230°, Reflex   **d)** 90°, Right

**6** 37°—Acute angle
   180°—Straight angle
   154°—Obtuse angle
   90°—Right angle
   279°—Reflex angle

**7 a)** 90°   **b)** 30°   **c)** 45°   **d)** 150°   **e)** 240°   **f)** 105°

**Challenge**

**b)** reflex

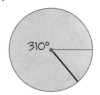

**c)** obtuse

**d)** acute

**e)** obtuse

**f)** reflex

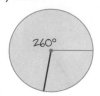

## 76-77 Symmetry

**Warm-up**

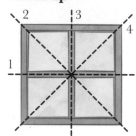

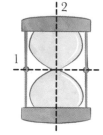

**Practice**

**1 a)**    **c)**    **e)**

**b)**    **d)**    **f)**

**2 a)** 5   **b)** 0   **c)** 1   **d)** 2

**3** a

**4 a)**    **b)**    **c)**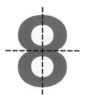

**Challenge**

150

**Warm-up**

**a)** reflection    **b)** translation    **c)** rotation

**Practice**

**1 b)**     **c)**     **d)**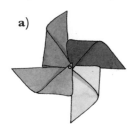

**2 a)** Translation    **b)** Reflection    **c)** Rotation

**3**

**a)**

**b)** 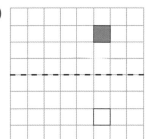    **c)**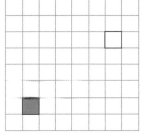

**4 a)** 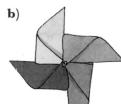    **b)**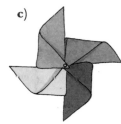

**5 a)**     **b)**

**6**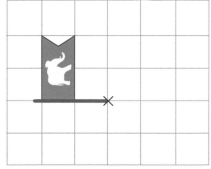

**7**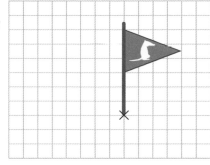

**Challenge**

**b)**

**c)**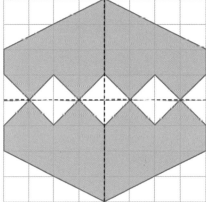

**d)**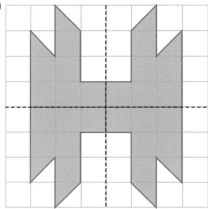

## 82–85 Lines

**Warm-up**

**a)** curved **b)** horizontal **c)** perpendicular **d)** vertical
**e)** diagonal **f)** parallel

**Practice**

1 Learner's own answers, but some examples are
given below.

**a)**

**c)**

**b)**

**d)**

2

| H | 2 | 2 | 4 |
|---|---|---|---|
| V | 1 | 2 | 3 |
| D | 5 | 7 | 4 |
| | | | |

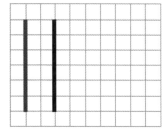

3 Learner circles a, h, and i.

4 Learner circles e and g.

5 Learner's own answers, but some examples are
given below.

**b)**

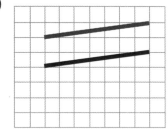

**c)**

**d)**
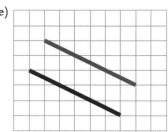

**e)**
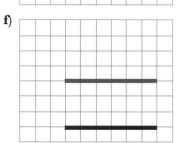

**f)**

6 Learner circles a, c, d, and e.

7 Learner draws a picture using straight and curved lines.

8 Learner draws a picture using parallel and
perpendicular lines.

9 From shortest to longest: b, d, f, c, a, e

10

**Challenge**

Learner draws a picture that uses at least four pairs of
perpendicular lines and three horizontal lines.

## 86–87 2D shapes

**Warm-up**

b, d, e, and f are polygons

**Practice**

1 **b)** Hexagon **c)** Heptagon **d)** Quadrilateral
**e)** Octagon **f)** Pentagon **g)** Nonagon

2 **a)** Triangle **b)** Heptagon **c)** Decagon
**d)** Quadrilateral **e)** Nonagon

## Challenge

**a**) A regular polygon with 4 corners
**b**) An irregular polygon with 4 sides
**c**) An irregular polygon with 5 angles
**d**) A regular polygon with 8 sides

## 88-89 Triangles

### Warm-up

### Practice

**1** a

**2** a

**3 a**) Learner draws a red circle around the blue triangle.
   **b**) Learner draws a black circle around the green triangle.

**4 a**) Right triangle
   **b**) Isosceles triangle
   **c**) Equilateral triangle
   **d**) Scalene triangle

### Challenge

Learner's own answers.

## 90-91 Angles in triangles

### Warm-up

Learner's own answers.

### Practice

**1** 25°

**2 a**) 45° **b**) 25° **c**) 30°

**3 a**) 57° **b**) 49° **c**) 49° **d**) 50° **e**) 35° **f**) 60°
   **g**) 60° **h**) 66° **i**) 66° **j**) 45°

**4 a**) 63° **b**) 71° **c**) 27° **d**) 70° **e**) 81° **f**) 27°

**5** b, e, g, and i do not describe a triangle

### Challenge

a = 42°
b = 48°

## 92-93 Quadrilaterals

### Warm-up

**a**) Parallelogram **b**) Trapezoid **c**) Rectangle
**d**) Rhombus **e**) Kite

### Practice

**1** a, c, d, g, h, and i are quadrilaterals

**2** Learner draws a rhombus with sides equal to 3 squares on the grid; for example:

**3** a, c, and f have four right angles

**4 b**)

**c**)

**d**)

**e**)

**f**)

**5 a**) 180° **b**) 2 x 180° = 360°

### Challenge

**a**) 70° **b**) 100° **c**) 90°

## 94-97 Circles

### Warm-up

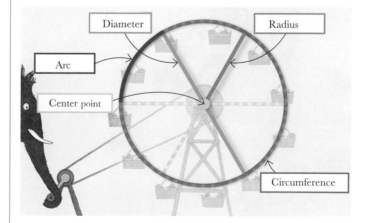

153

## 94-97 Circles (continued)

**Practice**

1  **a)** Distance all the way around the circle
   **b)** Distance from center of circle to circumference
   **c)** Distance across circle through center
   **d)** Part of the circumference

2  **a)** Radius      **b)** Diameter      **c)** An arc

  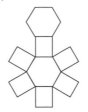

3

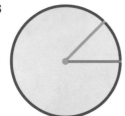

4  **b)** 20 x 3.14 = 62.8 m
   **c)** 60 x 3.14 = 188.4 mm

5  **a)** 31.4 cm   **b)** 37.68 cm   **c)** 56.52 cm   **d)** 47.1 m
   **e)** 65.94 m   **f)** 94.2 m

6  **a)** 52 mm   **b)** 36 cm   **c)** 55 cm   **d)** 27 m   **e)** 42 m
   **f)** 70 m

7  **a)** 204 m   **b)** 157 m   **c)** 104 m   **d)** 167 m

**Challenge**
Learner's own answers.

## 98-99 3D shapes

**Warm-up**
**a)** Hemisphere   **b)** Cylinder   **c)** Cuboid   **d)** Cube

**Practice**

1  **a)** Length   **b)** Height   **c)** Width   **d)** Face   **e)** Edge
   **f)** Vertex

2  **a)** Cuboid   **b)** Hemisphere   **c)** Pyramid   **d)** Sphere

3  **a)** 6   **b)** 3   **c)** 5   **d)** 6

4  **a)** 9   **b)** 8   **c)** 1   **d)** 1

**Challenge**
**a)** Sphere   **b)** Pyramid   **c)** Cuboid

## 100-103 Nets

**Warm-up**
**a)** Square   **b)** 6

**Practice**

1  **a)** Cylinder   **b)** Cuboid   **c)** Pyramid
   **d)** Triangular prism

2  a, c, e, f, and g are all nets of a square pyramid

3  **a)** i)  **b)** i)  **c)** iii)  **d)** ii)

4  a, d, e, and f are all nets of a cube

**Challenge**
**a)**

**b)** There are two possible nets.

## 104-105 Length

**Warm-up**
**a)** 7 m   **b)** 3.5 m   **c)** 4 m

**Practice**

1  **a)** 4 cm   **b)** 2 cm   **c)** 3 cm   **d)** 2.5 cm   **e)** 4.5 cm

2  From smallest to largest:
   4 mm, 480 mm, 420 cm, 480 cm, 42 m

3  **b)** ÷ 10   **c)** ÷ 1,000   **d)** × 10   **e)** x 1,000   **f)** ÷ 100

4  5.5 m—5,500 mm—550 cm
   5,000 mm—5 m—500 cm
   1.5 m—1,500 mm—150 cm
   3.2 m—320 cm—3,200 mm

**Challenge**
**a)** 1,400 m   **b)** 0.48 m   **c)** 37 m   **d)** 0.15 m   **e)** 6,800 m
**f)** 3,900 m

## 106-107 Perimeter

**Warm-up**
**b)** 6 + 6 + 6 + 6 = 24 cm
**c)** 15 + 20 + 15 + 20 = 70 cm
**d)** 18 + 18 + 18 = 54 mm

**Practice**

1  **a)** 18 m   **b)** 18 m   **c)** 26 m

2  **a)** 2a + 2b   **b)** 2a + b   **c)** 4a   **d)** 5b

3  **a)** Learner circles the green quadrilateral.
   **b)** Learner circles the green quadrilateral.
   **c)** Learner circles the red triangle.

**Challenge**
The elephant shrew is correct. The heptagon and the triangle have the same perimeter (21 cm), but the pentagon does not (20 cm).

## 108-111 Area

**Warm-up**

The whole garden is 6 m².

**Practice**

**1 a)** 14   **b)** 18   **c)** 12   **d)** 24

**2 a)** 12   **b)** 11   **c)** 14   **d)** 11   **e)** 7   **f)** 11

**3** Learner's own answers.

**4** 49 squares

**5 a)** $4 \times 2.5 = 10$ km²
  **b)** $2.6 \times 2.6 = 6.76$ cm²
  **c)** $3 \times 3 = 9$ mm²
  **d)** $12 \times 5.5 = 66$ cm²
  **e)** $8 \times 45 = 360$ mm²
  **f)** $5.4 \times 5.4 = 29.16$ km²

**6 a)** 5 cm
  **b)** $b \times 6 = 48$, $48 \div 6 = b$, $b = 8$ cm

**7 a)** 15 cm²   **b)** 3 cm²   **c)** 6 cm²   **d)** 20 cm²

**8 a)** 9 cm²   **b)** 12 cm²   **c)** 7 cm²   **d)** 18 cm²   **e)** 9 cm²
  **f)** 7.5 cm²

**Challenge**

This piece of cheese can feed 9 shrews.

## 112-115 Maps and coordinates

**Warm-up**

**a)** (E, 1)   **b)** (I, 2)   **c)** (A, 1)   **d)** (G, 2)

**Practice**

**1** Parachute—(H, 7)
  Elephant shrew—(G, 9)
  Duck pond—(I, 5)
  Mud bath—(C, 8)
  Bird—(H, 10)

**2 a)** (A, 3)   **b)** (C, 4)   **c)** (F, 3)   **d)** (I, 7)

**3 b)** Northeast   **c)** East   **d)** Southeast   **e)** South
  **f)** Southwest   **g)** West   **h)** Northwest

**4 a)** north   **b)** east   **c)** northeast   **d)** northwest

**5 b)** (A, 1)   **c)** (B, 5)   **d)** (C, 2)

**Challenge**

**a)** Rocky Mountains   **b)** Boulder Beach
**c)** (I, 10)   **d)** (C, 4)

## 116-117 Volume

**Warm-up**

**a)** 9 cm   **b)** 8 cm   **c)** 8 cm   **d)** $9 \times 8 \times 8 = 576$ cm³

**Practice**

**1 a)** 27   **b)** 20   **c)** 60   **d)** 12   **e)** 8

**2 b)** 800 ml   **c)** 300 ml

**3 a)** 64 cm³   **b)** 72 km²   **c)** 60 m³   **d)** 30 cm²

**4 a)** 120 cm³   **b)** 60,000 mm³   **c)** 42 cm³   **d)** 120 m³
  **e)** 72 km³   **f)** 54 mm³

**5 a)** 24 cm³   **b)** 512 mm³   **c)** 70 km³

**Challenge**

1,750 ml

## 118-119 Speed

**Warm-up**

**a)** 100 meters   **b)** 25 seconds

**c)**
$$\frac{\boxed{100}\ \text{m}}{\boxed{25}\ \text{s}} = \boxed{4}\ \text{m/s}$$

**Practice**

**1 a)** 5 m/s   **b)** 6 h   **c)** 6 h   **d)** 8 m/s

**2** 5 m/s

**3** 5 h

**4** 3 h

**5** 30 km/h

**6 a)** 72 s   **b)** 102 s

**Challenge**

**a)** 1 m/s
**b)** 2 m/s

## 120-121 Weight and mass

**Warm-up**

**a)** 15 kg   **b)** 5 mg   **c)** 10 g   **d)** 6 metric tons
**e)** From lightest to heaviest: ant, shrew, snake, mammoth

**Practice**

**1** 5 kg—5,000 g
  1 ton—1,000 kg
  300,000 g—3 metric tons
  200 mg—0.2 g

**2 a)** weight   **b)** mass   **c)** weight

**3 a)** Hamster   **b)** Parrot   **c)** Rabbit   **d)** Cat   **e)** Dog

**4 a)**

| Animal | Mass (g) | Mass (kg) |
|--------|----------|-----------|
| Shrew 2 | 6 | 0.006 |
| Shrew 3 | 7.5 | 0.0075 |
| Shrew 4 | 28 | 0.028 |
| Shrew 5 | 17 | 0.017 |

**b)**

| Animal | Weight on Earth (N) |
|--------|---------------------|
| Shrew 2 | 0.06 |
| Shrew 3 | 0.075 |
| Shrew 4 | 0.28 |
| Shrew 5 | 0.17 |

**Challenge**

| Animal | Mass on Earth (kg) | Weight on Earth (N) | Weight on Moon (N) | Difference (N) |
|---|---|---|---|---|
| Elephant shrew | 0.9 kg | 9 | 1.44 | 7.56 |
| Mammoth | 5,500 kg | 55,000 | 8,800 | 46,200 |
| Pigeon | 0.51 kg | 5.1 | 0.816 | 4.284 |
| Snake | 15 kg | 150 | 24 | 126 |

## 122-123 Temperature

**Warm-up**

Thermometers a, c, and e show temperatures above 50°F (10°C).

**Practice**

1   Room temperature—68°F
Boiling water—212°F
Ice cubes—32°F

2   **a)**           **c)**

    **b)**           **d)**

3   **a)** Antarctica   **b)** Greenland   **c)** Finland   **d)** Germany
    **e)** Japan   **f)** Brazil   **g)** Australia

4   Almut, Mia, and Apeksha should be treated for a fever.

**Challenge**

5°F

## 124-127 Telling time

**Warm-up**

There are 24 hours in 1 day, but only **12** hours on an analog clock. When the short hand points up at **12**, it is either midday or **midnight**. The short hand goes all the way around the clock twice in **one** day. There are **60** minutes in 1 hour. There are **60** seconds in 1 minute.

**Practice**

1   **b)**          **c)**

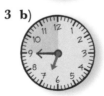 

2   **b)**          **c)**

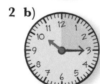 

3   **b)**      **c)**      **d)**

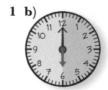  

4   **a)**     **b)**     **c)**     **d)**

5   **a)** 8:00   **b)** 2:30   **c)** 4:05   **d)** 4:35   **e)** 10:15   **f)** 6:45

6   **a)** 2:45   **b)** 3:00   **c)** 3:10   **d)** 3:25

7   12:30 p.m.—12:30
    12:30 a.m.—00:30
    5:00 p.m.—17:00
    9:30 a.m.—09:30
    1:45 p.m.—13:45

**8**

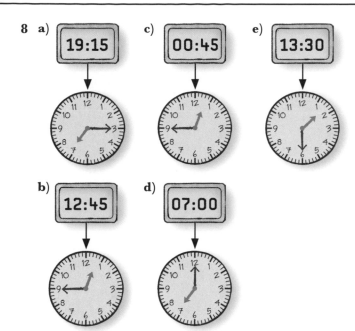

**9** **a)** The order of the clocks from left to right: 1, 5, 4, 2, 3
**b)** The order of the clocks from left to right: 2, 4, 1, 5, 3

**Challenge**

| Mammoth | Time taken in hours and minutes |
|---------|--------------------------------|
| 1 | 1 hour |
| 2 | 1 hour 30 minutes |
| 3 | 45 minutes |
| 4 | 55 minutes |
| 5 | 1 hour 25 minutes |

Mammoth 3 was the fastest.

## 128-129 Gathering data

**Warm-up**

| Bird | Tally |
|------|-------|
| Crow | // |
| Finch | /// |
| Magpie | / |
| Pigeon | /// |

**Practice**

**1** **a)** 11 **b)** 27 **c)** 29 **d)** 18

**2** **a)**

| | Finch | Sparrow | Pigeon | Crow |
|------|-------|---------|--------|------|
| Shrew 1 | | /// | /// | |
| Shrew 2 | // | //// | ⊬⊦⊦ / | |
| Shrew 3 | | | ⊬⊦⊦ // | / |
| Total number | // | ⊬⊦⊦ // | ⊬⊦⊦ ⊬⊦⊦ ⊬⊦⊦ / | / |

**b)** Pigeon

**Challenge**

Learner's own answers.

## 130-133 Graphs and charts

**Warm-up**

**a)** Saturday **b)** 20
**c)** Four days: Sunday, Monday, Wednesday, Thursday

**Practice**

**1**

| Day | Number of birds |
|-----|-----------------|
| Sunday | 15 |
| Monday | 30 |
| Tuesday | 20 |
| Wednesday | 25 |
| Thursday | 35 |
| Friday | 15 |
| Saturday | 10 |

**2**

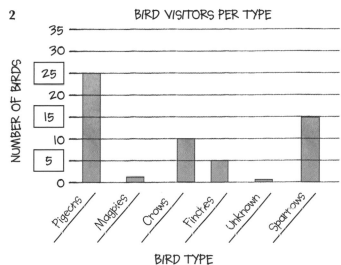

**3** **a)** 4 **b)** 2 **c)** 7 a.m., 8 a.m. **d)** 1

**4** **a)**

**b)** January, February, June **c)** 1,400

**5** **a)** Pigeon **b)** Magpie **c)** Sparrow

**6**

| | Number | Fraction | Percentage |
|---|---|---|---|
| Magpie | 12 | $^3/_{10}$ | 30% |
| Sparrow | 10 | $^1/_4$ | 25% |
| Finch | 6 | $^8/_{20}$ | 40% |
| Crow | 2 | $^1/_{20}$ | 5% |
| Total | 40 | 1 | 100% |

**Challenge**

| Activity | Percentage | Number of shrews |
|---|---|---|
| Soccer | 26% | 50 x 26 = 1,300<br>1,300 ÷ 100 = 13 shrews |
| Gym | 16% | 50 x 16 = 800<br>800 ÷ 100 = 8 shrews |
| Dance | 10% | 50 x 10 = 500<br>500 ÷ 100 = 5 shrews |
| Volleyball | 6% | 50 x 6 = 300<br>300 ÷ 100 = 3 shrews |
| None | 2% | 50 x 2 = 100<br>100 ÷ 100 = 1 shrew |

## 134-135 Venn diagrams

**Warm-up**

**Two** shrews like both soccer and ice hockey.
**Two** shrews don't like any of these sports.
**Three** shrews like all three activities.
**Three** shrews only like ice hockey.
**One** shrew likes ice hockey and snorkeling.
**Three** shrews only like snorkeling.

**Practice**

**1 a)** 4   **b)** 2   **c)** 15   **d)** 5   **e)** 10
**2** Even numbers: 6, 12, 18
Prime numbers: 3, 11, 19
Both even numbers and prime numbers: 2

**Challenge**

Swims: Shrew 3, Shrew 4
Plays soccer: Shrew 5, Shrew 6
Both swims and plays soccer: Shrew 1, Shrew 2
Outside the diagram: Shrew 7, Shrew 8

## 136-139 Averages

**Warm-up**

**a)** 13.5 m; 13.5 ÷ 5 = 2.7 m
**b)** The heights in order are 1.5 m, 1.5 m, 3 m, 3.5 m, and 4 m.
The median height is 3 m.
**c)** 1.5 m
**d)** 4 m − 1.5 m = 2.5 m

**Practice**

**1 a)** 6.6 cm   **b)** 2.6 cm   **c)** Windy Bay
**d)** Lake Splendid   **e)** 5 cm   **f)** 8 cm   **g)** 6 cm
**h)** 5 cm   **i)** 5 cm and 8 cm   **j)** 12 cm   **k)** 5 cm
**2 a)** 68 g—Median
62 g—Mean
50 g—Mode
**b)** 38 g
**3 a)** 2.2 m   **b)** 1.6 m   **c)** 2.5 m
**4 a)** Group 3   **b)** Group 2   **c)** 0.9 m
**5**

| Day | Number of birds | Mode |
|---|---|---|
| Monday | 10, 4, 4, 12, 3, 2, 7, 6 | **4** |
| Tuesday | 10, 15, 4, 10, 18, 17, 15, 8, 7 | **10, 15** |
| Wednesday | 18, 7, 12, 10, 10, 16, 20, 21 | **10** |
| Thursday | 12, 8, 7, 5, 5, 10, 16, 8 | **5** |

**6 a)** Popcorn: 50¢, Drink: 20¢, Ice cream: 69¢
**b)** Ice cream

**Challenge**

**a)** 253
**b)** Mean: 120, Median: 101, Mode: 100
**c)** Mean: 101, Median: 101, Mode: 100
**d)** The mean is much higher with the outlier included,
but the median and mode are both the same.

## 140-143 Probability

**Warm-up**

**a)** $^1/_6$   **b)** $^1/_{12}$   **c)** $^1/_4$   **d)** $^1/_2$

**Practice**

**1 a)** Equal chance   **b)** Impossible   **c)** Unlikely
**d)** Definite   **e)** Likely
**2 a)** 10   **b)** 4   **c)** $^4/_{10}$   **d)** $^2/_5$   **e)** $^3/_{10}$
**3** A number greater than 4—Impossible
Purple number 4 card—Unlikely
A card with an odd number—Equal chance
A number less than 5—Definite
A card that is not white—Likely
**4 a)** $^4/_{20} = {}^1/_5$   **b)** $^5/_{12}$
**c)** Area 2 (probability is ½)
**5 a)** $^{60}/_{120} = {}^1/_2$   **b)** $^{30}/_{120} = {}^1/_4$
**c)** $^{24}/_{120} = {}^1/_5$

**6 a)**

First dice

|  | 1 | 2 | 3 | 4 | 5 | 6 |
|---|---|---|---|---|---|---|
| **1** | 2 | 3 | 4 | 5 | 6 | 7 |
| **2** | 3 | 4 | **5** | 6 | 7 | 8 |
| **3** | 4 | **5** | 6 | **7** | 8 | 9 |
| **4** | 5 | 6 | 7 | 8 | 9 | 10 |
| **5** | 6 | 7 | **8** | 9 | 10 | 11 |
| **6** | 7 | 8 | 9 | 10 | 11 | **12** |

Second dice

**b)** $1/36$   **c)** $6/36 = 1/6$   **d)** 3   **e)** $3/36 = 1/12$   **f)** total of 9

**Challenge**

| Time | Chance of snow | Probability of snow |
|---|---|---|
| 7 a.m. | 70% | $70/100 = 7/10$ |
| Noon | 95% | $95/100 = 19/20$ |
| 4 p.m. | 22% | $22/100 = 11/50$ |
| 9 p.m. | 52% | $52/100 = 13/25$ |

The publisher would like to thank the following for their kind permission to reproduce their photographs:
**Dreamstime.com:**
Yuls2000 (All pages)
All other images © Dorling Kindersley Ltd.